Brenda Hopkin

DESERET
BOOK

Design and photo art direction by Shauna Gibby. Photography by John Luke and Alan Blakely

Photostyling by Maxine Bramwell

Library of Congress Cataloging-in-Publication Data

Lion House bakery.

   p. cm.

   Includes index.

   ISBN 978-1-60641-137-7 (hardbound : alk. paper)

 1. Baking.   I. Lion House (Restaurant)

   TX763.L565 2009

   641.8'15—dc22

                                                                            2009022807

Printed in the United States of America

Publishers Printing, Salt Lake City, UT

10 9 8 7 6 5 4 3 2 1

CONTENTS

Lion House Dinner Rolls

ROLLS AND BREADS

LION HOUSE DINNER ROLLS

2 cups warm water (110 to 115 degrees)
⅔ cup nonfat dry milk
2 tablespoons active dry yeast
¼ cup granulated sugar
2 teaspoons salt
⅓ cup butter, shortening, or margarine
1 egg
4½ to 5 cups all-purpose flour or bread flour
½ cup butter, melted

In a large bowl of an electric mixer, combine water and dry milk powder, stirring until milk dissolves. Add yeast, then sugar, salt, butter, egg, and 2 cups of the flour. Mix on low speed until ingredients are wet. Increase mixer speed to medium and mix for 2 minutes. Add 2 cups flour; mix on low speed until ingredients are wet, then for 2 minutes at medium speed. (Dough will be getting stiff, and remaining flour may need to be mixed in by hand.) Add remaining flour, ½ cup at a time, and mix again until dough is soft, not overly sticky, and not stiff. (It is not necessary to use the entire amount of flour.)

Scrape dough off sides of bowl and pour about 1 tablespoon of vegetable oil all around sides of bowl. Turn dough over in bowl so it is covered with oil. (This helps prevent dough from drying out.) Cover with plastic wrap and allow to rise in warm place until doubled in size, about 1½ hours. Sprinkle cutting board or counter with flour and place dough on floured surface. Roll out and shape as desired. Place on greased or parchment-lined baking pans. Cover lightly with plastic wrap. Let rise in warm place until rolls are doubled in size, about 1 to 1½ hours.

Bake at 375 degrees for 15 to 20 minutes, or until golden brown. Brush with melted butter while hot. Serve with Honey Butter or Raspberry Honey Butter. Makes 1½ to 3 dozen rolls, depending on shape and size of rolls.

Note: This recipe can be doubled, tripled, or even quadrupled if you have a large enough bowl.

You can also freeze shaped rolls for later use: Simply double the amount of yeast used when making dough. After the first rise, shape the rolls but do not rise again. Instead, place rolls on a baking sheet and immediately place in freezer. When dough is frozen solid, remove rolls from pan and place in a plastic bag, squeeze excess air out of bag and seal. Rolls can be frozen for 3 weeks.

BAKING INSTRUCTIONS FOR FROZEN ROLL DOUGH

Suggested Method

Spray a 9 x 13-inch baking pan with nonstick cooking spray. Place rolls evenly apart in four rows, three rolls in each row with the edge down and facing the same direction. Cover lightly with plastic wrap.

Let rolls rise for 3 to 5 hours, until double in size. Actual time will depend on the temperature of your kitchen.

Preheat the oven to 375 degrees. Carefully remove plastic wrap. Bake rolls 15 to 18 minutes, or until golden brown.

Remove rolls from oven and brush with melted butter.

Speed Method

Place rolls in pan same as suggested method. Do not cover. Preheat oven to 200 degrees. Boil 1 quart of water and place in a shallow pan on bottom rack of oven. Place pan of frozen rolls on the top rack.

Let dough rise about 1 hour, or until double in size. Do not allow dough to rise too high. Rolls will raise more as they bake. Remove rolls from oven and preheat the oven to 375 degrees. Bake rolls 15 to 18 minutes, or until golden brown.

Remove rolls from the oven and brush with melted butter.

After baking and cooling rolls, place in plastic bags. Rolls may be frozen or stored in the refrigerator for 4 days.

Reheating suggestions: Allow frozen baked rolls to thaw. Remove rolls from plastic bag, place in a brown paper bag and roll the opening closed. Sprinkle the outside of the paper bag with water. Place in a preheated 325-degree oven for 10 minutes. Serve immediately. Reheating in the microwave is not recommended.

Honey Butter

½ cup butter, softened
½ cup honey
¼ teaspoon vanilla

Beat butter until it is broken up. Add the honey and the vanilla. Beat for 10 minutes, scraping mixture to the bottom twice during the mixing. (It is very important that this mix for the entire 10 minutes or it will separate.) Store, refrigerated, in a plastic container.

Raspberry Honey Butter

½ cup butter, softened
¼ cup honey
¼ cup red raspberry preserves
¼ teaspoon vanilla

Beat butter until soft; add honey and preserves while mixer is running. Add vanilla and beat for 10 minutes. Store, refrigerated, in a plastic container.

Helpful Tips for Making Rolls

· Always add flour gradually and keep dough as soft as you can handle.

· It is not necessary to use the entire amount of flour listed in the recipe—add only enough flour to make a manageable dough. A soft dough will produce a lighter roll.

· To shorten dough's rising time, use one of these methods: (1) When dough is thoroughly mixed, oil bowl and cover dough with plastic. Fill sink or larger bowl with about 2 inches of hot water or enough water to come about half or three-quarters of the way up the outside of bowl. Place bowl of dough in bowl of water and allow to rise until doubled in size. (2) Just before mixing dough, heat oven to lowest possible temperature. Place a pan of hot water on bottom oven rack. When dough is thoroughly mixed, place in an oiled bowl and cover with plastic wrap. Put bowl in oven on the rack above the pan of water. Turn oven off, shut oven door, and allow dough to rise until doubled in size. Shape or cut into desired rolls. Place rolls on greased or parchment-lined pans and allow to rise until doubled in size. Bake according to recipe.

Both quick-rise methods may also be used for the second rise after shaping and placing rolls in pans. For method 1, fill sink or bowl halfway with hot water, place pan of shaped rolls across hot water. Allow rolls to rise until doubled in size and bake according to recipe. (Be sure pan will fit across water-filled sink or large bowl so that rolls do not fall in the water.) For method 2, reheat oven while shaping rolls. Place fresh pan of hot water in oven with pan of rolls. Turn off oven and shut door. Allow rolls to rise until half again the size they were when shaped. Remove from oven and preheat oven for baking. When rolls are double the size when shaped, bake according to recipe.

· Brush tops of rolls with butter when first removed from oven.
· To consistently make attractive, great-tasting rolls, practice! practice! practice!

Shaping Lion House Dinner Rolls

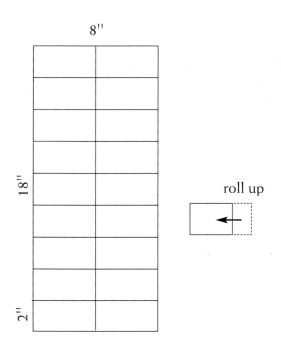

Rolls can be formed into many shapes and sizes. At the Lion House, we follow this method, which yields 18 large rolls: After allowing dough to rise until doubled in size, scrape out dough onto floured counter or cutting board. Turn dough over so it is floured on both sides and gently flatten to about 1-inch thick. With rolling pin, roll out to a rectangle 18 inches long, 8 inches wide, and ¼ of an inch thick. Brush with melted butter. With pizza cutter or very sharp knife, cut dough in half vertically to make two strips about 4 inches wide and 18 inches long. Make cuts through strips of dough every 2 inches, making about 18 pieces of dough.

Starting with short end, roll up one piece of dough with butter on the inside. Place roll on parchment-lined pan with other short end down on the paper. Repeat with remaining pieces of dough. Be sure all rolls face the same direction on baking pan.

Dilly Casserole Bread

POTATO ROLLS

½ cup warm water

2 tablespoons active dry yeast

1 tablespoon granulated sugar

1 cup milk, scalded

¾ cup shortening

½ cup granulated sugar

1 teaspoon salt

1 cup mashed potatoes (homemade or
    instant, instructions on package)

2 eggs, beaten

3 cups all-purpose flour

In a large bowl, combine water, yeast, and the 1 tablespoon sugar and set aside to proof. Scald milk in a small saucepan over medium heat. Remove from heat and add shortening, ½ cup sugar, and salt. Let cool. Once milk mixture is cool, add to yeast mixture, along with mashed potatoes, beaten eggs, and 1½ cups of the flour. Gradually add remaining flour until a soft dough forms. Cover bowl with plastic wrap and let rise until doubled, about 45 minutes.

Roll out dough on floured surface, shape rolls as desired, and place on greased pans. Cover with plastic wrap and let rise until doubled in size, 30 to 40 minutes.

Bake at 425 degrees for 15 minutes, or until golden brown. Turn out on cooling racks and brush with melted butter or margarine. Recipe makes 2 dozen rolls and can be doubled nicely.

LION HOUSE WHEAT ROLLS

1 package (2¼ teaspoons) active dry yeast

3 cups lukewarm water

1 cup quick-cooking rolled oats

¼ cup molasses

6 tablespoons nonfat dry milk

1 cup all-purpose flour

6½ cups whole wheat flour

6 tablespoons shortening

1½ tablespoons salt

Dissolve yeast in ¼ cup of the lukewarm water and set aside. In a large mixing bowl, combine remaining 2¾ cups water, oats, molasses, and dry milk powder; add half of the white flour and half of the whole wheat flour, one cup at a time, beating well after each addition. Add dissolved yeast, the remaining flour, shortening, and salt. Mix well, then knead until dough is smooth and elastic, about 5 minutes. Place in a covered bowl in a warm area until dough has doubled in bulk, about 1 hour. Knead for one minute to force out air bubbles. Pinch off and shape into 1¼-inch pieces and place on greased cookie sheets 1½ inches apart. Cover with plastic wrap and let rise until doubled in size, about 30 to 40 minutes.

Bake at 375 degrees for 12 to 15 minutes. Makes 4 dozen rolls.

OUT-OF-THIS-WORLD ROLLS

2 tablespoons active dry yeast

¼ cup warm water

½ cup granulated sugar

½ cup shortening

3 eggs

1 cup warm water

1½ teaspoons salt

4 to 5 cups all-purpose flour

Combine yeast and the ¼ cup warm water in a small bowl and set aside to proof. In a large mixing bowl, cream together sugar and shortening until light and fluffy. Add eggs, one at a time, mixing after each addition. Add softened yeast, 1 cup warm water, salt, and enough flour to make a soft dough. Mix well. Cover bowl with plastic wrap and let dough rise 1 hour. Punch down, let rise again for 40 to 45 minutes. Shape as desired and place on greased baking sheets. Cover with plastic wrap and let rise until doubled in size, about 40 minutes. Bake at 350 degrees for 15 minutes. Dough will keep in the refrigerator up to 5 days after second rise and shaping. Take out 3 hours before baking. Allow to rise for about 3 hours and bake as above.

This recipe makes 3 dozen small rolls.

BROCCOLI CHEDDAR ROLLS

1 recipe dough for Lion House Dinner
    Rolls, prepared through first rise
    (see pages 1–2)

1 (10-ounce) bag frozen chopped
    broccoli, thawed and drained

1 cup grated cheddar cheese

¼ cup dried minced onions

1 egg

1 teaspoon onion salt

2 tablespoons grated Parmesan cheese

2 tablespoons butter, melted

1 teaspoon Lawry's Seasoned Salt®

After dough for Lion House Dinner Rolls has completed first rise, turn out onto a floured surface. Roll out dough into a large rectangle, about ¼-inch thick. Mix broccoli, cheddar cheese, onions, egg, onion salt, Parmesan cheese, and Lawry's Seasoned Salt in a small bowl. Spread broccoli mixture over dough. Tightly roll up the dough jelly roll style. Using a little water on fingertips, pinch edge firmly to seal dough. Cut dough into 24 slices.

Place slices, cut side up, in cavities of muffin pans sprayed with cooking spray or place on greased baking sheets. Brush panned dough with melted butter. Cover with plastic wrap and let rolls rise until doubled in size, about 1 to 1½ hours. Bake at 375 degrees for 10 to 15 minutes. Remove from pan immediately to cool on a wire rack. Makes 2 dozen rolls.

Broccoli Cheddar Rolls

Cinnamon Rolls

CINNAMON ROLLS

2½ cups water

½ cup vegetable oil

3 eggs

1 teaspoon vanilla

½ cup nonfat dry milk

2 tablespoons active dry yeast

1 cup granulated sugar

1 tablespoon salt

7 cups all-purpose flour

½ cup sugar

2 teaspoons ground cinnamon

½ cup butter, melted

1 recipe Powdered Sugar Icing or
     Buttercream Frosting (see below)

Place water, oil, eggs, vanilla, and dry milk powder in the large bowl of an electric stand mixer and stir vigorously until milk is dissolved. Sprinkle yeast over liquid mixture, then add the 1 cup sugar, salt, and flour.

Put dough hook on mixer and mix for 10 to 15 minutes at low speed. The dough will be very sticky. Cover bowl with plastic wrap and let rise until doubled in size, about 1½ hours. Turn dough out onto a well-floured surface and roll out into a rectangle shape. Brush with melted butter. Sprinkle with sugar and cinnamon. Roll up rectangle lengthwise and cut into 1-inch slices. Grease a cookie sheet or line with parchment paper. Place rolls on cookie sheet, cover with plastic wrap, and allow to rise until doubled in size, 1 to 1½ hours.

Bake at 375 degrees for 12 to 14 minutes. After baking, let rolls cool slightly before frosting. Frost with Powdered Sugar Icing or Buttercream Frosting. Makes about 18 rolls.

Note: If you want to make the dough a day ahead, mix dough according to directions. Instead of allowing dough to rise, place it in an oiled bowl, cover with plastic wrap, and refrigerate overnight. When ready to use, remove dough from refrigerator and follow directions for rolling out, rising, and baking. It will take longer for the shaped rolls to rise because dough will be cold.

Powdered Sugar Icing

2 cups powdered sugar

1 teaspoon vanilla

¼ cup half and half or evaporated milk

Mix all ingredients together in a small mixing bowl and beat until light and well mixed.

Buttercream Frosting

3 cups powdered sugar

½ cup butter, softened

6 to 8 tablespoons cream or
     evaporated milk

1 teaspoon vanilla

Blend powdered sugar, butter, and 3 tablespoons of the cream in a large bowl with an electric mixer on low speed until combined well. Slowly add the rest of the cream, 1 tablespoon at a time, until creamy and smooth, but not at all runny. Add vanilla and mix again.

ORANGE ROLLS

1 recipe dough for Lion House Dinner
    Rolls, prepared through first rise (see
    pages 1–2)
½ cup butter, melted, plus additional
    butter for brushing hot rolls
Zest of two oranges
¼ cup granulated sugar
1 recipe Orange Glaze (see below)

After dough for Lion House Dinner Rolls has completed the first rise, punch down and turn out onto a floured surface. Roll out dough into a rectangle about 18 inches long, 8 inches wide, and ¼ of an inch thick. In a small bowl, combine ½ cup melted butter and orange zest. Brush dough with orange butter and sprinkle the ¼ cup sugar on top.

With pizza cutter or very sharp knife, cut dough in half vertically to make two strips about 4 inches wide and 18 inches long. Make cuts through strips of dough every 2 inches, making about 18 pieces of dough.

Starting with short end, roll up one piece of dough with orange butter on the inside. Place on lightly greased baking sheet and cover with plastic wrap. Allow to rise until doubled in size, 1 to 1½ hours. Bake at 375 degrees for 12 to 15 minutes, or until light golden brown. Remove from oven and brush with melted butter. Allow to cool about 10 to 15 minutes, then drizzle with Orange Glaze. Makes 18 rolls.

Orange Glaze

1½ cups powdered sugar
2 tablespoons orange juice, squeezed
    from 2 oranges
2 to 4 tablespoons heavy cream, or
    2 tablespoons half and half
1 to 2 teaspoons orange zest (optional)

Place powdered sugar and orange juice in bowl and add half the amount of heavy cream. With spoon or mixer, stir until smooth. If icing is too thick, add more cream a little at a time. (The hotter the rolls are when frosted, the thicker the frosting needs to be.) If desired, add 1 to 2 teaspoons orange zest.

CHEESY PULL APART ROLLS

1 cup butter, melted

¾ cup grated Parmesan cheese

12 frozen rolls, thawed, or 1 recipe dough for Lion House Dinner Rolls, prepared through first rise (see pages 1–2)

Combine melted butter and Parmesan cheese in a shallow bowl. Cut thawed frozen rolls in half the short way. Roll each dough piece in the cheese and butter mixture. Place in a well-greased Bundt pan. Or, if using dough for Lion House Dinner Rolls, shape ⅔ of the dough into 24 small dough balls (see recipe note below); roll dough balls in cheese and butter mixture and place in a well-greased Bundt pan. Cover pan and allow dough to rise until it is doubled in size, 35 to 40 minutes. Bake at 375 degrees for 20 to 25 minutes. Invert onto serving platter after cooling for 10 minutes. Serves 10 to 12.

Note: If using Lion House Dinner Roll dough, follow recipe as outlined on page 1. After dough has completed the first rise, divide into 3 portions. Use 2 portions to shape rolls for this recipe and 1 portion to make a loaf of bread.

POLYNESIAN COCONUT ROLLS

1¾ cups coconut milk

1 cup water

6 tablespoons sugar

4 teaspoons cornstarch

12 frozen rolls, thawed, or 1 recipe dough for Lion House Dinner Rolls, prepared through first rise (see pages 1–2)

Combine coconut milk, water, sugar, and cornstarch in a small bowl, stirring well until cornstarch is dissolved. Coat a 9 x 13-inch baking pan with cooking spray. Pour mixture into pan.

Place thawed rolls on top of coconut mixture. Or, if using dough for Lion House Dinner Rolls, divide dough into 3 portions and shape 2 of those portions into 12 rolls; place rolls on top of coconut mixture. Cover pan with plastic wrap and allow rolls to rise until doubled in size, about 1 to 1½ hours. Bake at 375 degrees for 20 minutes. These are best served hot. Makes 1 dozen rolls.

Note: If using Lion House Dinner Roll dough, follow recipe as outlined on page 1. Divide dough into 3 sections after first rise. Use 2 portions to shape rolls for this recipe and 1 portion to make a loaf of bread.

Caramel Rolls

CARAMEL ROLLS

1 recipe dough for Lion House Dinner
    Rolls, prepared through first rise (see
    pages 1–2)

½ cup butter, melted

1 cup packed brown sugar

1 (6-ounce) package vanilla pudding mix
    (not instant)

3 tablespoons milk

½ cup chopped nuts

½ teaspoon ground cinnamon

¼ cup sugar (mix with cinnamon)

After dough for Lion House Dinner Rolls has completed the first rise, turn dough out onto floured board or counter and divide into 3 equal portions. Coat a 9 x 13-inch pan or large Bundt pan with nonstick cooking spray. Tear 1 portion of dough into small pieces and drop randomly in bottom of pan. Combine melted butter, brown sugar, pudding mix, milk, nuts, and cinnamon in a small bowl. Stir until well blended. Pour ⅔ of this mixture over the dough pieces in pan. Tear second portion of dough into pan to fill in empty spots. Pour remaining sauce over dough pieces; sprinkle with cinnamon-sugar. (Use remaining portion of dough to bake a loaf of bread.) Cover with plastic wrap and allow to rise in warm place until doubled in size, 45 minutes to 1 hour. Bake at 375 degrees for 30 minutes. Allow to cool 10 minutes, then invert onto large platter. Serves 8 to 10.

Note: Any frozen bread dough may be substituted for Lion House Dinner Rolls dough. Allow 2 loaves of frozen dough to thaw; use one loaf for bottom layer and one for top layer. It may take a bit longer for dough to rise using this method. If using Lion House Dinner Roll dough, follow recipe as outlined on pages 1–2. Divide dough into 3 portions after first rise. Use 2 portions to shape rolls for this recipe and 1 portion to make a loaf of bread.

APPLE CINNAMON BUNS

¾ cup chopped walnuts or almonds

2 medium cooking apples, pared, cored,
    and thinly sliced

2 teaspoons ground cinnamon

12 frozen rolls, thawed, or 1 recipe
    dough for Lion House Dinner Rolls,
    prepared through first rise (see pages
    1–2)

1 (3-ounce) package vanilla pudding mix
    (not instant)

½ cup pancake or maple syrup

¼ cup butter, melted

Coat a 9 x 13-inch pan with nonstick cooking spray. Sprinkle with nuts then layer apple slices over bottom of pan. Roll thawed dough balls in cinnamon and arrange over almonds and apples. Or, if using dough from Lion House Dinner Rolls, divide dough into 3 equal portions and shape 2 of those portions into 12 dough balls; roll in cinnamon and arrange over almonds and apples. Sprinkle dry pudding mix over dough balls and drizzle with the syrup and butter. Cover with a clean towel or plastic wrap and let rise until doubled in size, 1 to 1½ hours. Bake at 375 degrees for 20 to 30 minutes. Invert pan onto serving plate. Serves 12.

Note: If using Lion House Dinner Roll dough, follow recipe as outlined on pages 1–2. Divide dough into 3 portions after first rise. Use 2 portions to shape rolls into 12 balls for this recipe and 1 portion to make a loaf of bread.

HOT CROSS BUNS

1½ cups milk

⅓ cup butter or margarine

5 cups all-purpose flour

⅓ cup granulated sugar

2 tablespoons active dry yeast

½ teaspoon salt

1 teaspoon ground cinnamon

½ teaspoon nutmeg

¼ teaspoon ground cloves

2 eggs

½ cup currants or candied fruit

1 egg white, lightly beaten

1½ cups powdered sugar

1 tablespoon water

½ teaspoon vanilla

In a small saucepan, heat milk and butter over medium heat, stirring constantly, until mixture is just warm and butter is melted. In a large mixing bowl, stir together 2 cups of the flour, sugar, yeast, salt, cinnamon, nutmeg, and cloves. Gradually add warmed milk; beat with electric mixer for 2 minutes. Beat in eggs. With a spoon, stir in currants or candied fruit and enough of the remaining flour to make dough easy to handle. Turn dough out onto a lightly floured surface; knead until smooth and elastic, about 5 minutes. Place in a greased bowl, turning once to grease top. Cover with plastic wrap and let rise until doubled in size, about 1 to 1½ hours.

Punch down dough. Divide into 4 equal parts. Cut each part into 6 equal parts. Shape each piece into a ball. Place about 2 inches apart on greased cookie sheets. Using a sharp knife, cut a cross on top of each ball. Cover and let rise until doubled in size, about 1 hour. Brush lightly beaten egg white over tops of buns. Bake at 350 degrees for 15 minutes, or until golden brown. Cool slightly.

Mix powdered sugar, 1 tablespoon water, and vanilla until smooth. Stir in additional water if needed. Drizzle over baked buns. Makes 2 dozen buns.

BUTTERY BREAD

12 frozen rolls, thawed, or 1 recipe dough for Lion House Dinner Rolls, prepared through first rise (see pages 1–2)

½ cup butter, melted

Cut each thawed roll in half the short way and place in a greased Bundt pan; let rise 2 to 3 hours. Alternatively, shape two-thirds of the dough for Lion House Dinner Rolls into small balls and place in greased Bundt pan.

When rolls have risen, bake at 375 degrees for 15 to 20 minutes, or until light brown on top. Immediately after removing from oven, pour melted butter over top. Let stand for a few minutes so butter can soak in. Invert onto serving platter and serve warm. Serves 8 to 10.

Seasoned Breadsticks

1 recipe dough for Lion House Dinner
    Rolls, prepared through first rise
    (see pages 1–2)
½ cup butter, melted
1 teaspoon poppy seeds
1 teaspoon sesame seeds
½ teaspoon fennel seeds
½ teaspoon caraway seeds
⅛ teaspoon celery seed, cumin, or
    dill seeds

After dough for Lion House Dinner Rolls has completed first rise, turn out onto a floured surface. Roll dough into a large rectangle about ½-inch thick. Brush with melted butter; cut in desired widths and lengths (¾-inch wide and 4 to 5 inches long is ideal) and place on greased cookie sheet. In a small bowl, combine seasonings. Sprinkle over breadsticks.

Cover with plastic wrap and allow to rise until breadsticks are half again the size when rolled out, about 30 to 40 minutes. Bake at 375 degrees for about 10 minutes. Makes 30 breadsticks.

Note: If desired, you can leave the breadsticks plain or sprinkle with just poppy seeds, sesame seeds, or Parmesan cheese.

Jesse Evans Smith's 90-Minute Bread

2 cups warm water (105 to 115 degrees)
2 tablespoons active dry yeast
2 teaspoons salt
¼ cup granulated sugar
3 tablespoons vegetable oil
4 to 5 cups all-purpose flour

Grease two 5 x 9-inch loaf pans. Set aside.

Pour water into a large bowl and sprinkle yeast over it. Sprinkle sugar and salt over yeast and wait until yeast bubbles and comes to the surface. Stir in oil. Add 2½ cups of the flour and whisk smooth with a wire whisk (or wooden spoon). Add 2 more cups of the flour and mix until dough gathers together in a ball. Sprinkle the remaining flour on work table. Turn dough onto it and knead in flour until the dough is no longer sticky but is elastic and slightly stiff, about 10 minutes. Divide dough into two loaves. Shape each loaf and place into greased bread pans; lightly cover with plastic wrap. Let dough rise until it peeks over the edge of the pan or doubles in bulk, about 45 minutes. Place in a 375-degree oven for 30 to 35 minutes, or until brown. Turn loaves out on a rack to cool. Brush tops with butter while hot.

Challah Braid and Hot Cross Buns

WHOLE WHEAT BREAD

1 package (2¼ teaspoons) active dry yeast

3 cups lukewarm water

1 cup oatmeal

¼ cup molasses

6 tablespoons nonfat dry milk

6 tablespoons shortening

5½ cups whole wheat flour

1½ tablespoons salt

2 cups white all-purpose flour

Directions for mixing with electric mixer: Soften yeast in 3 cups lukewarm water in a large mixing bowl. Add remaining ingredients and beat until dough forms a ball and leaves sides of bowl (part of flour may need to be mixed in by hand). Remove beaters, cover bowl, and let dough rise for 1 hour in a warm place, away from drafts. Punch down and shape into 2 loaves. Place in 2 well-greased 5 x 9-inch loaf pans; cover with a clean towel and let rise until almost doubled in size, about 45 minutes. Bake at 350 degrees for 30 minutes, or until a deep golden brown. Turn loaves out onto a wire rack to cool. Brush tops with melted butter. Makes 2 loaves.

Directions for hand mixing: Dissolve yeast in ¼ cup lukewarm water and set aside. Combine remaining 2¾ cups water, oats, molasses, and dry milk powder; add half the white flour and half the whole wheat flour, one cup at a time, beating well after each addition. Add softened yeast, remaining flour, shortening, and salt. Mix well; knead until dough is smooth and elastic, about 5 minutes. Place in a covered bowl in warm place until doubled in size. Knead 1 minute to force out air bubbles. Shape into two loaves. Place in 2 well-greased 5 x 9-inch loaf pans. Cover and let rise until doubled in size. Bake at 350 degrees for 30 minutes. Remove from pans to cool. Brush tops of loaves with melted butter.

CHALLAH BRAID

1 tablespoon dry yeast

1½ cups water (110 to 115 degrees)

¼ cup granulated sugar

¼ cup vegetable oil

1 teaspoon salt

2 eggs, beaten well

Pinch of saffron (optional)

4½ to 5 cups flour

1 egg yolk, beaten well

¼ teaspoon water

Sesame seeds

Place yeast and water in a large bowl. Stir slightly to dissolve. Add sugar, oil, salt, beaten eggs, saffron, and 2½ cups flour. Beat well. Add enough remaining flour to make a soft dough and knead until smooth. Place in a greased bowl. Cover and let rise until double in bulk (30 to 40 minutes). Punch down dough and divide into 6 pieces. Roll each piece into a long rope, 18 to 20 inches long and 1 inch in diameter. Braid three of the ropes together. Repeat with the remaining 3 pieces of dough. Place on a greased cookie sheet. Mix egg yolk with ¼ teaspoon water and brush over braids. Sprinkle with sesame seeds. Cover and let rise 30 minutes. Bake at 375 degrees about 30 to 35 minutes. Makes 2 braids.

QUICK AND EASY FRENCH BREAD

2 cups hot water
2 tablespoons shortening
2 tablespoons granulated sugar
4 teaspoons salt
2 packages active dry yeast
1 cup lukewarm water
7 to 8 cups all-purpose flour
Evaporated milk
Coarse salt or sesame seeds

Combine the 2 cups hot water, shortening, sugar, and salt in a large bowl. Stir to melt shortening and dissolve sugar and salt. Set aside and cool to lukewarm.

Dissolve yeast in 1 cup lukewarm water. Add to cooled shortening-sugar mixture.

Mix in 4 cups of the flour and beat until well blended. Add remaining flour to make moderately stiff dough and knead until well mixed.

Cover and place in a warm spot to rise until doubled, about 1 hour.

Punch down and divide into 4 balls. Let rise for 10 minutes.

Roll each ball into a rectangle then roll up as a jelly roll. Shape and seal the ends. Score with kitchen shears or a sharp knife down the top of the loaf. Place on greased cookie sheets (2 per sheet), brush with evaporated milk and sprinkle with coarse salt or sesame seeds.

Cover and allow to rise for 1½ hours, or until almost doubled.

Bake at 400 degrees for 25 minutes. Brush with melted butter, if desired, and remove to wire racks to cool.

Makes 4 small loaves.

PARMESAN BREAD

4 cups warm water
4 tablespoons active dry yeast
¼ cup granulated sugar
¼ cup butter, softened
4 teaspoons salt
1 cup grated Parmesan cheese
7¼ cups all-purpose flour

Sprinkle yeast over the water in a large bowl. Let stand a few minutes, then stir to dissolve. Add sugar, butter, salt, all but 1 tablespoon of the Parmesan cheese, and 6 cups of the flour. Beat at low speed until smooth. Beat in remaining 1¼ cups flour. Cover the bowl and allow to rise for 45 minutes. Stir bread down and beat 25 strokes with a wooden spoon. Pour into a lightly greased, 2-quart oven-proof bowl and sprinkle with reserved 1 tablespoon Parmesan cheese. Bake at 375 degrees for 45 to 55 minutes, or until nicely browned.

WHOLE WHEAT BRAN BREAD

1 cup all-purpose flour
1 cup whole wheat flour
1 cup All-Bran® cereal
1 tablespoon granulated sugar
1 teaspoon salt
1 package (2¼ teaspoons) active dry yeast
¾ cup milk
1 tablespoon molasses
3 tablespoons butter or margarine
1 egg
Melted butter or margarine

In a small mixing bowl, stir together flours. In the large bowl of an electric mixer, combine ½ cup of the flour mixture, the All-Bran cereal, sugar, salt, and yeast. Set aside.

In a small saucepan, combine milk, molasses, and the 3 tablespoons butter. Place over low heat until very warm (120 degrees). Gradually add to cereal mixture and beat at medium speed of electric mixer for 2 minutes, scraping bowl occasionally.

Add egg and ¼ cup of the flour mixture. Beat at high speed 2 minutes. With spoon, stir in remaining flour mixture to make a stiff dough. Turn dough out onto lightly floured surface and knead for 5 minutes, or until smooth and elastic. Place in well-greased bowl, turning to grease top. Cover and let rise in a warm place about 1 hour, or until doubled in size.

Punch dough down. Form into smooth round ball with hands, being careful not to create large folds in dough. Place on a greased baking sheet. Cover and let rise in a warm place about 1 hour, or until doubled in size.

Bake at 375 degrees about 30 minutes, or until golden brown. Remove immediately from baking sheet. Place on a wire rack and brush with melted butter. Cool. Makes 1 round loaf.

DILLY CASSEROLE BREAD

1 package (2¼ teaspoons) active dry yeast

¼ cup lukewarm water

1 cup cottage cheese, heated to lukewarm

2 tablespoons granulated sugar

2 tablespoons finely chopped onion or
    1 tablespoon dried minced onion

1 tablespoon butter or margarine, soft-
    ened, plus additional butter for
    brushing hot bread

1 tablespoon dill weed

1 teaspoon salt

¼ teaspoon baking soda

1 egg

2¼ to 2½ cups all-purpose flour

Soften yeast in water in a small bowl and set aside. In a mixing bowl, combine cottage cheese, sugar, onion, 1 tablespoon butter, dill weed, salt, baking soda, egg, and softened yeast. Add flour to form a stiff dough, beating well after each addition. Cover and let rise in a warm place, until light and doubled in size, about 50 to 60 minutes. Punch dough down. Turn into a well-greased, 1½- to 2-quart round casserole. Cover and let rise in a warm place for 30 to 40 minutes. Bake at 350 degrees for 40 to 50 minutes, or until golden brown. Brush with soft butter and sprinkle with salt. Makes 1 round loaf.

LION HOUSE RAISIN BREAD

1 recipe dough for Lion House Dinner
    Rolls, prepared through the addition
    of remaining flour (see pages 1–2)

2 cups raisins

1½ teaspoons active dry yeast

¾ teaspoon ground cinnamon

¾ teaspoon nutmeg

Prepare dough for Lion House Dinner Rolls, stirring in raisins, yeast, cinnamon, and nutmeg at the same time that remaining flour is mixed into dough. Scrape down dough from sides of bowl. Pour a little oil around edge of bowl. Turn dough over once in bowl so dough is covered with oil. Cover with plastic wrap and allow to rise until doubled in size, 45 to 55 minutes. Shape into 2 loaves and place in greased 5 x 9-inch loaf pans. Allow to rise until dough is 1 inch above edge of pan, about 35 to 40 minutes. Bake at 350 degrees for 25 to 30 minutes, or until golden brown. Brush with melted butter after removing from oven; remove from pans and cool on wire rack. Makes 2 loaves.

Lion House Raisin Bread and Whole Wheat Bread

OATMEAL BREAD

5¾ to 6¼ cups all-purpose flour

2 tablespoons active dry yeast

1¾ cups water

1 cup quick-cooking rolled oats,
    plus more for baking

½ cup light molasses

⅓ cup shortening

1 tablespoon salt

2 eggs

1 egg white, beaten (optional)

1 tablespoon water (optional)

In a large mixer bowl, combine 2 cups of the flour and the yeast and set aside. In a saucepan, heat the 1¾ cup water, the 1 cup rolled oats, light molasses, shortening, and salt until just warm (115 to 120 degrees) and shortening is almost melted; stir constantly. Add to flour mixture. Add the 2 eggs. Beat at low speed of an electric mixer for half a minute, scraping sides of bowl constantly. Beat 3 minutes at high speed. Stir in as much of the remaining flour as you can mix with a spoon. Turn out onto a lightly floured surface. Knead in enough of the remaining flour to make a moderately soft dough that is smooth and elastic, 3 to 5 minutes total. Shape into a ball. Place in a lightly greased bowl; turn once to grease surface. Cover and let rise in a warm place until doubled in size, about 1½ hours.

Punch down dough and turn out onto a lightly floured surface. Divide dough in half. Cover and let rest 10 minutes. Grease two 9 x 5 x 3-inch loaf pans. If desired, coat each pan with rolled oats.

Shape dough into loaves. Place loaves in pans. Cover and let rise until nearly doubled in size, 45 to 60 minutes. If desired, brush loaves with mixture of egg white and 1 tablespoon water; sprinkle tops lightly with additional rolled oats. Bake in a 375-degree oven for 40 to 45 minutes. Cover loosely with foil the last 15 minutes of baking to prevent overbrowning. Remove from pans and cool on a wire rack. Makes 2 loaves.

ONION CHEESE BREAD

1½ cups chopped onion

3 tablespoons butter

2 to 3 cloves garlic, minced (optional)

1 recipe dough for Lion House Dinner Rolls, prepared through second addition of flour (see pages 1–2)

1 cup grated Parmesan cheese

1 tablespoon vegetable oil

Melt 3 tablespoons butter in a large skillet over medium-high heat. Add onions and garlic and cook and stir until onion is translucent. Remove from heat and allow mixture to cool completely.

Prepare dough for Lion House Dinner Rolls, adding cooled onion mixture and Parmesan cheese after addition of 4th cup of flour. Mix on low speed until thoroughly blended. Add one more cup of flour and mix on low speed until moistened. At this point the flour may need to be kneaded in. Place remaining flour on countertop and scrape dough out onto the flour. Knead together until dough is a little soft, but not runny or sticky. (Additional flour may be needed.)

Place 1 tablespoon oil in a large bowl and spread all over the bowl. Place dough in bowl and turn over once. Cover bowl with plastic wrap and place in a warm place. Allow to rise until doubled in size, about 1 to 1½ hours. Coat two baking sheets with nonstick cooking spray.

When dough has doubled in size, work the dough down with your hands. Cut dough in half and form into two round balls. Place each round on a greased cookie sheet, cover, and allow to rise until doubled in size. Bake in a 350-degree oven for 30 to 35 minutes. Brush with butter while warm. Turn onto wire racks to cool. Makes 2 rounds.

BREAD FACTS

Flour: The amount of flour needed in each recipe will vary according to the humidity of the environment. The quantity mentioned in the recipe is only approximate. The main difference between flours is their protein content.

Liquid: For good bread, it is necessary to produce a creamy texture. Milk, water, or potato water may be used. Water is the only liquid in many fine breads, such as French and Italian. Bread made with milk is more nutritious, has a browner crust, and will keep longer. Potato water makes a slightly larger loaf and coarser bread. Skim milk powder may be used in place of regular milk to provide more nutrition and convenience.

Sugar: Sugar helps brown the crust and also helps the yeast to work properly. Try granulated, light brown, dark brown, or raw sugar interchangeably. Honey and molasses will add moisture and flavor to your bread.

Salt: Salt gives flavor and stabilizes yeast fermentation. The usual proportion is 1 teaspoon for every 2 cups of flour.

Fat: Butter, margarine, shortening, vegetable oil, bacon fat, or lard may be used. Butter makes bread tender and gives it a nice flavor.

Eggs: Eggs add flavor, color, and delicacy to yeast doughs. Egg yolks make the finest dough for sweet breads and coffee cakes. In recipes calling for egg yolks alone, the whole egg can be substituted. Simply use 1 whole egg for each 2 yolks called for. The opposite also holds true. Simply add 2 egg yolks for each 1 egg called for.

Baking: Bread, when baked and done will be an even, rich brown color. However, if you are not sure about doneness, turn the loaf out of the pan onto a bread board. Tap the bottom of the loaf lightly with a knuckle. If the bread is done, there will be a distinctly hollow sound. If you do not hear this, turn the bread back into the pan and bake a short time longer.

Additions: Be daring and add something new to your dough, such as cinnamon and raisins, chocolate chips, dates, Parmesan cheese, sautéed garlic or onions, orange or lemon zest, your favorite herbs, ham and cheese, or your favorite jam or preserves. Roll the dough flat and spread with peanut butter and jelly; roll dough up and bake it.

Form: Bake the bread in different shapes—in a loaf (there are hundreds of different size pans), in a casserole dish of any shape, in empty cans, as a round or square or whatever shape you can think of on a sheet.

Finishing Touches: Brush bread with an egg wash (one egg whisked with 2 tablespoons of water or milk) before baking. Sprinkle with sesame seeds, poppy seeds, herbs, coarse ground pepper, or sea salt. For a crustier crust, spritz water into the oven after putting your loaves in to bake. A lower oven temperature (350 degrees) will give you a thicker crust.

11 Tips for Homemade Bread

1. Never let your baking become monotonous. Try a new recipe. Make different sized and shaped loaves and rolls.

2. If your kitchen is cool, set the bowl of dough on a heavy plate over a bowl of warm water. Never let the outside of the dough bowl become more than comfortably warm to the hand.

3. A poor job of kneading the dough before the first rising period cannot be remedied.

4. Never add all the flour the recipe calls for to the dough while it is in the bowl. Save ½ to 2 cups of flour, depending on the size of the recipe, to use while kneading the dough on the pastry board.

5. Bread making is a skill, and its results depend on the cook's deftness in mixing, kneading, letting dough rise, and baking.

6. Bread is economical because it gives a high return in food value for what it costs.

7. When bread dough is doubled in bulk and ready to bake, a slight indentation made with the finger will remain.

8. When making wheat bread, add ⅛ to ¼ teaspoon ginger. It is a yeast improver. (You get more volume from the yeast.)

9. When freezing unbaked bread or rolls, add ⅓ or ½ more yeast than the recipe calls for. Dough will hold in the freezer for 2 weeks.

10. When freezing unbaked bread or rolls, always shape the dough and put directly in the freezer. Do not allow to rise after it is shaped.

11. Bake large batches of bread. Allow to cool completely then slice (an electric knife works best). Place slices in plastic bags, gently squeeze the excess air out, twist-tie the bag closed, and freeze. It's ready to use anytime.

Breakfast Pizza

SAUSAGE ROLL UPS

 QUICK & EASY

2 loaves frozen bread dough, thawed but not risen

1 (10½-ounce) package frozen spinach

1 pound Italian sausage, skinned and cooked

½ pound pepperoni slices, cut in half

½ medium onion, chopped and sautéed

1 cup grated Swiss cheese

½ cup grated Parmesan cheese

Salt and pepper to taste

Garlic powder

Preheat oven to 375 degrees. Roll out both loaves of dough and press onto a greased 15 x 11-inch baking sheet. Pinch seams together and set aside.

Place spinach in a small amount of boiling water in a medium pan; cover and remove from heat. Allow to stand for 5 minutes, then drain.

Sprinkle dough with spinach, sausage, pepperoni, onions, and cheeses. Season with salt, pepper, and garlic powder, to taste. Roll dough up jelly roll style. Allow to rise 30 minutes. Bake 20 to 25 minutes, until bread is browned and filling is hot.

Note: One recipe dough for Lion House Dinner Rolls (see pages 1–2) can be used in place of the frozen dough, if desired.

BREAKFAST PIZZA

1 pound pizza dough*

1 pound pork sausage, cooked and drained

2 medium potatoes, grated, or 2 cups frozen hash brown potatoes

½ cup chopped green or red bell pepper (optional)

½ cup chopped onion (optional)

1 cup grated Monterey Jack cheese

4 eggs

½ cup milk

½ teaspoon salt

Preheat oven to 375 degrees. Roll out dough and place on a well-greased 18 x 13-inch jelly roll pan. Sprinkle pork sausage and grated potatoes over dough. If using, sprinkle chopped green or red pepper and onion over sausage and potatoes. Cover top with grated cheese. In a small bowl, blend eggs, milk, and salt with a wire whisk and pour over top of cheese. Bake 20 to 25 minutes. Serves 12.

*Note: Fresh pizza dough can be purchased at the deli counter of most grocery stores or at your local pizzeria. As a substitute, you can thaw 12 frozen dough rolls prepared using the Lion House Dinner Rolls recipe on pages 1–2. Thaw rolls, unroll, and press each together to form a single crust.

CHEESE STRATA

6 to 8 Lion House Dinner Rolls, sliced,
or 12 slices bread

3 cups grated cheese (Cheddar, Swiss,
Monterey Jack)

2 cups diced ham

6 eggs

3½ cups milk

2½ teaspoons dried onion flakes

½ teaspoon salt

¼ teaspoon dry mustard

Layer half of the sliced rolls on the bottom of greased
9 x 13-inch pan. Sprinkle 2 cups of the grated cheese over the
rolls. Cover with diced ham. Top with the other half of the
sliced rolls. In a medium bowl, beat eggs with milk, onion
flakes, salt, and mustard. Pour over the rolls. Cover with
plastic wrap and refrigerate overnight. Bake, uncovered, at
350 degrees for 40 minutes. Remove from oven, add remaining 1 cup cheese, and return to oven for
15 more minutes. Serves 8 to 10.

*Note: Instead of using ham, try cooked and crumbled sausage. Or, try adding spinach,
red and yellow bell peppers, or broccoli.*

SWISS ONION RING

 QUICK
& EASY

2 cups shredded Swiss cheese

6 tablespoons butter, melted

½ cup finely chopped green onion or
¼ cup chopped yellow onion

2 tablespoons poppy seeds

¼ teaspoon salt

12 frozen rolls, thawed, or 1 recipe
dough for Lion House Dinner Rolls
prepared through first rise

Preheat oven to 375 degrees. In a medium bowl, combine
grated cheese, butter, onions, poppy seeds, and salt and set
aside. Cut thawed rolls in quarters. Arrange half of the dough
pieces in bottom of well-greased ring mold or tube pan.
Cover dough with half of the cheese mixture. Top with
remaining dough pieces. Spread remaining cheese mixture on
top. Or, if using dough from Lion House Dinner Rolls,
divide dough into 3 sections after first rise. Shape 2 of those
sections into 48 small dough balls and use in place of the
thawed roll quarters. Cover loosely with plastic wrap and rise
until doubled. Bake 18 minutes, cover with foil and bake an
additional 3 to 5 minutes. Remove from the oven, loosen
edges with a sharp knife, invert pan on a plate, and remove
pan immediately. Serve cool or warm.

*Note: If using Lion House Dinner Rolls dough, follow recipe as outlined on pages 1–2,
divide dough into 3 portions after first rise. Use 2 portions to shape rolls into tiny balls
for this recipe and 1 portion to make a loaf of bread.*

QUICK BREADS AND MUFFINS

BANANA-NUT BREAD

6 large or 8 medium bananas, very ripe

4 eggs

2 cups granulated sugar

¾ cup vegetable oil

4 cups all-purpose flour

1 teaspoon baking soda

2 teaspoons salt

2 teaspoons baking powder

½ cup chopped walnuts

Grease and flour two 8 x 4-inch loaf pans and set aside. Preheat oven to 325 degrees.

Peel bananas and place in a large mixing bowl; mash bananas well. Add eggs, sugar, and oil and mix until well blended. In a separate bowl, mix flour, baking soda, salt, and baking powder. Add to banana mixture. Mix until blended. Add nuts and mix briefly. Do not overmix. Pour into prepared pans. Bake 45 to 50 minutes, or until wooden toothpick inserted in center comes out clean. Turn loaves out onto wire racks to cool. Makes 2 loaves.

ZUCCHINI BREAD

3 cups all-purpose flour

1 teaspoon baking soda

½ teaspoon baking powder

2 teaspoons ground cinnamon

3 eggs

1 cup vegetable oil

2 cups granulated sugar

1 tablespoon vanilla

2 cups grated zucchini

1 cup chopped walnuts

Preheat oven to 325 degrees. Grease and flour an 8 x 4-inch loaf pan or two 7 x 3-inch loaf pans and set aside. In a large bowl, whisk together flour, baking soda, baking powder, and cinnamon and set aside. In a separate bowl, beat eggs with an electric mixer until light and foamy. Add oil, sugar, vanilla, and grated zucchini and mix well. Fold in flour mixture, stirring just until moist. Do not overmix. Fold in nuts.

Pour batter into prepared pan(s), about two-thirds full. Bake 45 to 50 minutes for large loaf or 35 minutes for smaller loaves, or until a toothpick inserted in center comes out clean. Turn loaves out onto wire racks to cool. Serves 10 to 12.

Nauvoo Café Bran Muffins

Nauvoo Café Bran Muffins

3 cups all-purpose flour

1 teaspoon salt

1 tablespoon baking soda

1¼ cups All-Bran® cereal

1¼ cups boiling water

1¼ cups dried cranberries

1¾ cups golden raisins

1¼ cups granulated sugar

¾ cup butter, softened

3 eggs

3½ cups Bran Flakes® cereal

1½ cups buttermilk

1¼ cups chopped walnuts

Preheat oven to 375 degrees. Grease and flour muffin top pans or regular muffin tins for 24 muffins.

Whisk together flour, salt, and baking soda and set aside. Place All-Bran cereal in a small bowl and cover with boiling water. Stir gently to moisten all of the cereal then set aside. Place dried cranberries and golden raisins in a small bowl and cover with hot tap water then set aside.

In a large mixing bowl, beat sugar and butter together until soft. Add eggs and beat until fluffy. Add dry ingredients and moistened All-Bran and mix until incorporated. Add Bran Flakes. Turn mixer on low and slowly add the buttermilk. Mix until all ingredients are well incorporated.

Drain dried cranberries and golden raisins, then fold into the batter along with chopped walnuts.

Scoop ¼ cup batter into each muffin cup. Bake 15 to 20 minutes. You can test for doneness by inserting a toothpick in the center of a muffin. If the toothpick comes out clean, the muffins are done.

Note: These taste even better when the batter is prepared a day in advance. The batter will keep two weeks in the refrigerator.

Lion House Pumpkin Bread

1½ cups vegetable oil

5 eggs

1 (16-ounce) can pumpkin

2 cups all-purpose flour

2 cups granulated sugar

1 teaspoon salt

1 teaspoon ground cinnamon

1 teaspoon nutmeg

1 teaspoon baking soda

1 (3-ounce) package vanilla instant pudding

1 cup chopped nuts

Preheat oven to 350 degrees. Grease and flour two 9 x 5-inch loaf pans and set aside.

Beat oil, eggs, and pumpkin in a large mixing bowl. In a separate bowl, sift together flour, sugar, salt, cinnamon, nutmeg, and baking soda. Add dry ingredients to pumpkin mixture and mix until well blended. Stir in pudding mix and nuts. Pour into prepared pans and bake for 1 hour. Test for doneness by sticking a toothpick in the loaf, just off center. If the toothpick comes out clean, the bread is done. Turn loaves out onto wire racks to cool. Makes 2 loaves.

CHERRY NUT BREAD

1 cup granulated sugar

½ cup vegetable oil

2 eggs

1 teaspoon vanilla

2¼ cups all-purpose flour

1 teaspoon baking powder

1 (8-ounce) jar maraschino cherries,
   chopped, juice reserved

½ cup chopped walnuts

Preheat oven to 325 degrees. Grease and flour two 9 x 5-inch loaf pans and set aside.

In a large mixing bowl, cream sugar and oil; add eggs and beat well. Stir in vanilla. In a separate bowl, whisk together flour and baking powder. Measure out ½ cup of the reserved maraschino cherry juice. (If juice does not equal ½ cup, add enough water to make up the rest.) Alternately add flour mixture and cherry juice to sugar mixture until all is well blended. Fold in cherries and nuts. Pour into prepared pans and bake 55 to 60 minutes, or until toothpick inserted near center comes out clean. Turn loaves out onto wire racks to cool. Dust with powdered sugar when cooled. Makes 2 loaves.

JANELL'S POPPY SEED BREAD

½ cup butter, melted

3½ tablespoons vegetable oil

2 eggs

½ cup milk

¾ cup granulated sugar

½ teaspoon vanilla

½ teaspoon almond extract

1 cup all-purpose flour

½ teaspoon salt

1 teaspoon baking powder

¾ teaspoon poppy seeds

1 recipe Orange Almond Icing (see
   below)

Preheat oven to 325 degrees. Grease and flour an 8 x 4-inch loaf pan and set aside.

In a large mixing bowl, cream together butter, oil, eggs, milk, sugar, vanilla, and almond extract. In a separate bowl, whisk together flour, salt, baking powder, and poppy seeds. Add dry ingredients to cream mixture until well blended but not over-mixed. Pour into prepared pan and bake for 45 minutes. Test for doneness by sticking a toothpick in the loaf, just off center. If the toothpick comes out clean, the bread is done. Turn loaves out onto wire racks to cool. Frost with Orange Almond Icing while still warm. Makes 1 loaf.

Orange Almond Icing

1 tablespoon orange juice

¼ teaspoon vanilla

¼ teaspoon almond extract

¼ cup powdered sugar

Mix all ingredients in a small bowl until well blended. Yields enough icing for 1 loaf bread.

Chocolate Zucchini Bread, Janell's Poppy Seed Bread, and Cherry Nut Bread

Angel Biscuits

ANGEL BISCUITS

1 package (2¼ teaspoons) active dry yeast

¼ cup warm water

5 cups all-purpose flour

1 teaspoon salt

¼ cup granulated sugar

2 teaspoons baking powder

1 cup shortening

2 cups buttermilk

3 tablespoons butter, melted

Preheat oven to 400 degrees and grease a cookie sheet.

Dissolve yeast in warm water and set aside. Measure all the dry ingredients and stir together. Cut in the shortening with a pastry cutter or two knives. Add yeast to the buttermilk, then add this to the first mixture. Mix well with a fork, wooden spoon, or your hands. Turn out on floured counter and pat to desired thickness. Cut biscuits with a round biscuit cutter or a glass cup. Dip biscuits in melted butter and place on greased pan. Bake 12 minutes, or until golden brown on top. Makes 18 biscuits.

Note: You may bake these at once or leave on the counter for a while (30 to 40 minutes) before baking. They can also be frozen, unbaked, if covered first with plastic wrap and then foil. To use, remove from freezer and allow to thaw completely. Remove wraps and bake as instructed above.

DATE NUT BREAD

1¼ cups all-purpose flour

1½ teaspoons baking soda

¾ teaspoon salt

⅔ cup chopped dates

⅔ cup boiling water

⅔ cup brown sugar, lightly packed

2½ tablespoons vegetable oil

2 eggs

½ cup chopped nuts

Preheat oven to 325 degrees. Grease and flour an 8x4-inch loaf pan; set aside.

In a medium bowl, whisk together flour, baking soda, and salt; set aside. Place chopped dates in a small bowl and cover with boiling water. Let dates cool to lukewarm. While dates are cooling, cream together brown sugar, oil, and eggs. Blend in date mixture. Stir in flour, then chopped nuts and mix well. Pour into prepared pan and bake 35 to 40 minutes. Test for doneness by sticking a toothpick in the loaf, just off center. If the toothpick comes out clean, it is done. Turn loaves out onto wire racks to cool. Makes 1 loaf.

RICH CORN BREAD

1 cup all-purpose flour

1 cup yellow cornmeal

1 teaspoon salt

4 teaspoons baking powder

4 eggs

½ cup sour cream

1 (16-ounce) can cream-style corn

2 tablespoons salad or vegetable oil

¾ cup grated cheddar cheese

Preheat oven to 400 degrees. Grease an 8 x 4-inch loaf pan or an 8 x 8-inch square pan and set aside. Sift together flour, cornmeal, salt, and baking powder and set aside. Beat eggs until light. Add sour cream, corn, and salad oil. Stir in dry ingredients and beat well. Pour into prepared pan and sprinkle with grated cheese. Bake 30 minutes. Test for doneness by sticking a toothpick in the loaf, just off center. If the toothpick comes out clean, the bread is done.

JOHNNY CAKES (CORNMEAL MUFFINS)

2 cups yellow cornmeal

1 cup all-purpose flour

1½ teaspoons salt

1½ teaspoons baking powder

¾ teaspoon baking soda

1 cup packed brown sugar

4 eggs, beaten

¾ cup butter, melted

1¼ cups sour cream

2 cups frozen corn, thawed

Preheat oven to 375 degrees. Coat 12 large muffin cups with nonstick cooking spray or line with cupcake papers and set aside.

In a large bowl, whisk together cornmeal, flour, salt, baking powder, baking soda, and sugar. In a separate bowl, beat eggs and stir in the sour cream. Pour egg mixture, melted butter, and corn into the dry ingredients and fold together. Do not overmix. Scoop batter into prepared muffin cups and bake 18 to 22 minutes, or until a toothpick inserted near center comes out clean. Makes 12 muffins.

Rich Corn Bread

Molasses Brown Bread

1 cup all-purpose flour

1 teaspoon baking soda

½ teaspoon salt

½ teaspoon ground cinnamon
   (optional)

1 egg

1 cup All-Bran® cereal

½ cup raisins

2 tablespoons shortening

⅓ cup molasses

¾ cup very hot water

Preheat oven to 350 degrees. Grease and flour a 9 x 5-inch loaf pan.

Whisk together flour, baking soda, salt, and cinnamon and set aside.

In a large mixing bowl, beat egg until light and foamy. Mix in All-Bran, raisins, shortening, and molasses. Add water, stirring until shortening is melted. Add dry ingredients, mixing only until combined.

Spread batter evenly in prepared pan and bake about 35 minutes. Bread is done when a toothpick inserted near center comes out clean. Remove from pan, let cool slightly on a wire rack, then slice and serve warm.

Chef's Biscuits

2 cups all-purpose flour

½ teaspoon salt

4 teaspoons baking powder

2 tablespoons granulated sugar

½ teaspoon cream of tartar

½ cup shortening

1 egg

¾ cup milk or buttermilk

Preheat oven to 400 degrees. In a large bowl, stir together flour, salt, baking powder, sugar, and cream of tartar. Cut in shortening with a pastry blender. Crack egg into a 1-cup measuring cup and stir with a fork. Pour milk in the cup with the egg, using enough milk to fill the cup. Stir first mixture slightly, then pour all the milk and egg in and stir together with a fork until all ingredients are combined. Handle carefully and not too much. Pat or roll out ½-inch thick. Cut with a biscuit cutter or glass and bake on a greased baking sheet 15 to 20 minutes. Makes 24 biscuits.

CHOCOLATE ZUCCHINI BREAD

2 cups all-purpose flour
½ teaspoon baking powder
1 teaspoon baking soda
1 teaspoon salt
½ teaspoon ground cinnamon
3 eggs
1 cup granulated sugar
1 cup brown sugar
1 cup vegetable oil
1 teaspoon vanilla
2 cups grated zucchini
2 ounces unsweetened chocolate, melted
1 cup semi-sweet chocolate chips

Preheat oven to 325 degrees. Grease and flour two 8 x 4-inch loaf pans and set aside.

Whisk together flour, baking powder, baking soda, salt, and cinnamon in a large bowl and set aside. In a separate mixing bowl, beat eggs with an electric mixer until light and foamy. Add the sugars, oil, vanilla, and melted chocolate and beat until creamy. Stir in grated zucchini. Mix in the dry ingredients until just incorporated. Do not overmix. Fold in chocolate chips. Pour equal amounts batter in each loaf pan and bake 45 to 50 minutes. Turn loaves out onto wire racks to cool. Makes 2 loaves.

PUMPKIN MUFFINS

1 spice cake mix
1 (15-ounce) can pumpkin
1 cup chocolate chips

Preheat oven to 350 degrees. Grease 24 muffin cups or fill 2 muffin tins with cupcake papers.

Mix all ingredients in a large bowl. Fill muffin cups two-thirds full and bake 16 to 18 minutes. Makes 24 muffins.

Pumpkin Cream Cheese Pie

PIES AND CRISPS

LION HOUSE PIE DOUGH

¼ cup butter

⅓ cup lard

¼ cup margarine

⅓ cup shortening

1 tablespoon granulated sugar

½ teaspoon baking powder

1 teaspoon salt

1 tablespoon nonfat dry milk

1½ cups pastry flour

1½ cups bread flour

½ cup plus 1 tablespoon cold water

Preheat oven to 375 degrees.

In a mixer, cream together butter, lard, margarine, and shortening. In a separate bowl, whisk together sugar, baking powder, salt, and dry milk powder; add to creamed butter mixture and mix briefly. Add pastry flour and beat until blended. Add bread flour and mix slightly. Pour in water and beat again just until water is blended.

Divide dough into two or three balls. Roll out each ball on a floured board. Line pie pan with dough and cut off excess dough. Flute edges. For recipes that call for baked pie crusts, prick holes in bottom with fork. Bake empty pie shell at 375 degrees for 12 to 15 minutes, or until light golden brown. Otherwise, fill unbaked pie shell and bake according to recipe. Makes 2 to 3 9-inch pie shells.

Note: You can substitute 3 cups all-purpose flour for the pastry and bread flour called for in the recipe. Additionally, this dough may also be made by hand-cutting the fats into the dry ingredients. This recipe can be used to make the crust for any recipe in this book that calls for a single- or double-crust pastry.

PASTRY FOR DOUBLE-CRUST PIE

2½ cups all-purpose flour
¼ cup granulated sugar
½ teaspoon salt
1 cup butter-flavored shortening, chilled
1 egg, beaten
1 tablespoon vinegar
¼ cup ice water

Preheat oven to 375 degrees.

In a medium bowl, mix together flour, sugar, and salt. Cut the shortening into the flour until pea-sized crumbs form. Carefully stir in beaten egg and vinegar. Gently sprinkle in water until dough starts to hold together. Shape dough into 2 disks. Use to make 2 single-crust pies or 1 double-crust pie. When recipe calls for a baked pie shell, roll out dough, press into pie plate, trim and flute edges, prick bottom of shell with a fork, and bake at 375 degrees for 15 to 20 minutes.

OATMEAL CRISP PASTRY DOUGH

4⅓ cups all-purpose flour
⅔ cup rolled oats (not quick oats)
½ teaspoon baking powder
½ teaspoon salt
1 tablespoon packed brown sugar
1½ cups shortening
½ cup cold unsalted butter, cut into
    small pieces
1 egg
1 tablespoon vinegar
Ice water

Stir together flour, oats, baking powder, salt, and brown sugar in a large bowl. Cut in shortening with pastry cutter or 2 knives. Add small pieces of butter and set aside. Mix together egg, vinegar, and enough ice water to measure 1 cup. Add to flour mixture. Mix well. Divide into four disks. Wrap with plastic wrap and refrigerate until ready to use. Makes enough dough for 2 double-crust pies or 4 single-crust pies.

HELPFUL TIPS FOR MAKING PIES

• For better sealing, brush edges of pie crusts with water just before putting on top crust.

• For a beautiful golden top, brush pie crust with milk, cream, half and half, or evaporated milk and sprinkle with sugar before baking.

• If your oven is large enough, bake 4 to 8 pies at a time and freeze in gallon freezer bags. When pies are frozen, stack them on top of each other. When needed, take pre-baked frozen pie out of plastic bag and bake at 325 degrees for 35 to 40 minutes.

• Keep pie shells from shrinking by pricking bottoms with a fork before baking. You can also prevent shrinking by lining dough with aluminum foil. Pour 2 to 3 cups dried beans, wheat, or rice into foil-lined shell and bake for half the baking time. Lift out foil and contents and continue baking for remainder of baking time.

• Experiment with different pastry recipes for your pie crusts. You may find that you prefer one over another or that one tastes best with fruit pies and another tastes better with cream pies.

ASSEMBLING AND BAKING FRUIT PIES

To assemble fruit pies, line a 9-inch pie plate with dough, pressing dough lightly against sides of pan and letting dough hang off over edges of pie tin. Spoon pie filling into unbaked shell. Brush edge of dough with water and place top crust on pie. Seal crusts together by gently pressing around the edge of pie tin. Cut excess dough from edge of pie. Crimp or flute edges if desired. Brush crust (but not edge) with milk, cream, half and half, or evaporated milk. Vent top crust and then sprinkle sugar on top and bake at 375 degrees for 45 to 50 minutes, or until crust is golden brown. If crust cracks open or filling comes out the sides, the pie is overdone.

BASIC CREAM PIE WITH VARIATIONS

4 cups milk

2 cups half and half

2 tablespoons butter

1¼ cups granulated sugar, divided

3 egg yolks

¼ teaspoon salt

½ cup cornstarch

1½ teaspoons vanilla

2 baked 9-inch pie shells (see page 41)

Whipped cream, for garnishing

Reserve up to 1 cup milk to mix with cornstarch later in the recipe. Place remaining milk in top pan of a double boiler; add half and half, butter, and ¾ cup of the sugar. Heat over medium high heat until butter is melted and milk is scalded.

In a small bowl, whisk egg yolks well; add remaining ½ cup sugar and salt and whisk very well. Slowly add egg mixture to hot milk mixture, stirring constantly for about half a minute; allow mixture to cook for 15 to 20 minutes, stir frequently. (This gives eggs time to cook and start thickening. Undercooking at this point can slow the finishing process by as much as half an hour.)

Mix reserved milk and cornstarch in a small bowl and slowly add to hot mixture, stirring constantly to avoid formation of lumps. Continue to stir for at least 2 minutes, then stir every 5 minutes for 15 to 20 minutes. When pudding is thick, stir in vanilla. Remove double boiler from stove. Pour half of the filling into each pie shell, rounding tops of pies. Cool on wire racks then chill in refrigerator 2 to 3 hours. Top with whipped cream when ready to serve. Makes 2 pies or 12 to 16 servings.

Coconut Cream Pie

Add 1 cup coconut (toasted, if desired) to pie filling with vanilla. Pour into baked shells. Chill 3 to 4 hours. When ready to serve, whip cream and spread over pie. Top each pie with another ¼ cup coconut.

Banana Cream Pie

Before pouring hot filling into pie shells, slice 2 bananas into each baked shell. Pour filling over bananas. Chill 3 to 4 hours. When ready to serve, whip cream and spread over pies.

Coconut Cream Pie

Chocolate Cream Pie

Add 1 cup to 1⅓ cups semi-sweet chocolate chips to hot pudding. Stir until melted. Pour filling into pie shells. Chill 3 to 4 hours. When ready to serve, whip cream and spread over pies.

Pralines and Cream Pie

Add 1 cup caramel ice cream topping and 1 cup chopped pecans to basic filling. Pour into baked pie shells. Chill 3 to 4 hours. Top with sweetened whipped cream before serving.

German Chocolate Pie

To hot filling, add 1½ cups semi-sweet chocolate chips, 1 cup coconut, ½ cup chopped pecans, and ½ cup caramel ice cream topping. Stir until well blended. Pour into baked pie shells.

Tropical Isle Pie

To hot filling, add 1 cup coconut, ⅔ cup drained, crushed pineapple, and ⅔ cup drained mandarin oranges. Pour into baked pie shells.

CARAMEL APPLE PIE

¾ cup granulated sugar, plus additional
    for dusting top crust

½ cup all-purpose flour

1 teaspoon ground cinnamon, plus addi-
    tional for dusting top crust

½ teaspoon kosher salt

1 large pinch nutmeg, plus additional for
    dusting top crust

8 apples, peeled, cored, and sliced

1 tablespoon vanilla

2 tablespoons unsalted butter

2 tablespoons cream

1 recipe Pastry for Double-Crust Pie
    (see page 42)

1 recipe Caramel Sauce (see below)

Preheat the oven to 375 degrees. In a large bowl, mix together sugar, flour, cinnamon, kosher salt, and nutmeg. Toss in apples, and stir in vanilla. Set aside. Stir the apple mixture every 15 to 20 minutes while making the crust.

Once pastry dough is prepared, roll out pastry for bottom crust 3 inches larger than the pie tin. Ease pastry into pan and cut away so only ½ an inch is overlapping the edge of the pie tin.

Pour apple filling into the pie pan. Dot the butter over the apples. Brush cream around edges of pie crust.

Roll out pastry for top crust, fold in half, and cut three ½-inch slits through both layers of crust. Unfold crust and place over the apples. Trim away extra crust, leaving 1 inch overlapping. Crimp edges of pie. Brush cream over top and sprinkle cinnamon, sugar, and nutmeg over top.

Cover the edges of the pie with foil. Bake for 1 hour and 20 minutes, or until lightly brown. Remove the tinfoil from edges after 30 minutes. Cover the whole pie with tinfoil for the last 20 minutes. Cool on a rack for 1 hour. While pie is cooking, make the caramel sauce. Drizzle warm sauce over pie before serving.

Caramel Sauce

¼ cup butter

1½ cups brown sugar

½ cup heavy cream

2 tablespoons corn syrup

1 teaspoon vanilla

In a heavy 2-quart saucepan, melt butter on high heat. Add brown sugar, heavy cream, and corn syrup. Bring to a boil, stirring frequently. Reduce heat to medium, until sauce thickens slightly, about 5 to 7 minutes. Remove from heat and add vanilla. Allow to cool in pan for 15 minutes. Drizzle over the warm pie.

Quick Swiss Apple Pie

Apple Pie

Pastry for a double-crust pie
(see page 42)

¾ to 1 cup granulated sugar

2 tablespoons all-purpose flour

½ to 1 teaspoon ground cinnamon

¼ to ½ teaspoon nutmeg

⅛ teaspoon salt

5 to 6 golden delicious apples, peeled,
cored, and sliced

2 tablespoons butter or margarine

Preheat oven to 375 degrees. Roll out pastry for bottom crust and line bottom and sides of pie tin. Roll out top crust, fold in half, and cut three ½-inch slits through both layers of crust, then set aside. In a large bowl, combine dry ingredients and stir. Place sliced apples on top of dry ingredients and stir. Pour apple mixture in bottom of pie crust. Dot with small pieces of butter. Moisten edge of pie crust with water. Place top crust on pie and seal. Brush with milk, sprinkle with sugar, and bake 45 to 50 minutes or until apples test tender when a sharp knife is inserted into vent hole on top of crust. Makes 6 to 8 servings.

Note: A 30-ounce can of apple pie filling may be substituted for fresh apples. Pour filling into pie crust. Sprinkle with cinnamon and nutmeg and dot with butter. Follow directions above for finishing pie.

Quick Swiss Apple Pie

Pastry for a double-crust pie
(see page 42)

1 (21-ounce) can cherry pie filling

1 (21-ounce) can apple pie filling

½ teaspoon ground cinnamon

¼ teaspoon nutmeg

Preheat oven to 375 degrees. Roll out pastry for bottom crust and line pie tin. Roll out top crust, and slash with a knife 4 to 6 times to vent, then set aside. Spoon cherries from cherry filling, leaving about ⅓ cup thickened juice in can, into bottom of pie shell. Gently spoon entire can of apple filling over cherries. Sprinkle with cinnamon and nutmeg. Moisten edge of pie crust with water. Add top crust and seal. Brush with milk and sprinkle with sugar. Bake for 35 to 45 minutes. Makes 6 to 8 servings.

CHERRY PIE

Pastry for a double-crust pie
 (see page 42)
2½ tablespoons quick-cooking tapioca
⅛ teaspoon salt
1 cup granulated sugar
3 cups water-packed red sour cherries,
 drained, with juice reserved
6 drops red food coloring
¼ teaspoon almond extract
1 tablespoon butter

Preheat oven to 375 degrees. Roll out pastry for bottom crust and line pie tin. Roll out pastry for top crust, fold in half, and cut three ½-inch slits through both layers of crust, then set aside. Combine tapioca, salt, and sugar in a large bowl. Measure ½ cup of the reserved cherry juice and add to bowl, along with cherries, food coloring, and almond extract. Mix well. Let stand about 15 minutes then pour into pie shell; dot with butter. Unfold top pie crust and place over pie; press top and bottom crusts together around edge. Crimp or flute. Bake 45 to 50 minutes. Makes 6 to 8 servings.

FRESH STRAWBERRY PIE

4 cups diced ripe strawberries
2 cups granulated sugar
½ teaspoon salt
½ cup cornstarch
½ teaspoon lemon zest
2 tablespoons freshly squeezed lemon
 juice
1 baked 9-inch pie shell (see page 41)
2 cups halved ripe strawberries
½ cup fresh blueberries
Whipped cream, for garnishing

Place diced strawberries in a gallon-sized zipper-top bag; seal well and knead bag to crush berries. Pour crushed berries into a large saucepan and combine with sugar and salt. Remove 1 cup of this mixture and blend with cornstarch in a small bowl; pour back into saucepan. Cook and stir strawberry mixture over medium-high heat until it comes to a boil. Reduce heat to medium and continue to stir and scrape the bottom of the pan until thick and clear. Stir in lemon zest. Place in a chilled, medium-sized bowl and cool in refrigerator, about 1 hour. Stir in lemon juice. Place halved strawberries and ¼ cup of the blueberries in bottom of baked pie shell. Spoon chilled glaze over berries. Garnish with whipped cream and remaining blueberries. Makes 6 to 8 servings.

Fresh Peach Pie

3 cups water

1 cup granulated sugar

1 (3-ounce) package peach flavored
gelatin

3 tablespoons cornstarch

4 cups sliced peaches

1 baked 9-inch pie shell (see page 41)

In a medium saucepan, bring water and sugar to a boil over medium high heat. Mix gelatin and cornstarch together and gradually add to the boiling sugar water. Cook over medium-high heat, stirring constantly for 5 minutes or until mixture is clear and thickened slightly; remove from heat. Let stand at room temperature until cool and thickened like a heavy syrup. (Or refrigerate to cool, stirring often, so it doesn't set up too much.) Pour over fresh peaches and fold together gently. Mound mixture in baked pie shell. Chill for at least 2 hours before serving. Top each slice with a dollop of whipped cream, if desired. Makes 6 to 8 servings.

Blueberry Pie

Pastry for a double-crust pie
(see page 42)

1 (16-ounce) bag frozen blueberries,
thawed

1 cup granulated sugar

¼ teaspoon salt

4 tablespoons cornstarch

Preheat oven to 375 degrees. Roll out pastry for bottom crust and line pie tin. Roll out pastry for top crust, fold in half, and cut three ½-inch slits through both layers of crust, then set aside. Pour thawed berries and juice into a large mixing bowl. In a separate bowl, mix sugar, salt, and cornstarch; pour on top of berries. Mix well with rubber spatula. Fill crust, add top crust, and bake 45 to 50 minutes, or until golden brown. Makes 6 to 8 servings.

VERY BERRY PIE

Pastry for 2 double-crust pies
    (see page 42)
1 (16-ounce) bag frozen boysenberries,
    thawed
1 (8-ounce) bag frozen blueberries,
    thawed
1 (8-ounce) bag frozen raspberries,
    thawed
1¾ cups granulated sugar
½ teaspoon salt
½ cup cornstarch

Preheat oven to 375 degrees. Roll out pastry for 2 bottom crusts and line 2 pie tins. Roll out pastry for 2 top crusts; fold each in half and cut three ½-inch slits through both layers of both crusts, then set aside. Pour thawed berries and all their juices into a large mixing bowl. In a separate bowl, mix sugar, salt, and cornstarch and pour on top of berries. Mix well with rubber spatula. Fill crusts, add top crusts, and bake 45 to 50 minutes, or until golden brown. Makes 2 pies or 12 to 16 servings.

DEEP-DISH PEACH AND SOUR CHERRY PIE

1 recipe Pastry for Double-Crust Pie
    (see page 42)
4 cups sliced fresh peaches
2 cups sour cherries
⅔ cup granulated sugar
1 tablespoon lemon juice
¼ cup packed brown sugar
3 tablespoons cornstarch
¼ teaspoon ground cinnamon

Crumb Topping:

1 cup all-purpose flour
½ cup rolled oats
⅔ cup packed brown sugar
½ teaspoon ground cinnamon
½ cup butter cut into ¼-inch pieces

Preheat oven to 400 degrees. Prepare pastry and roll three-fourths of the dough into a large round. Line a deep-dish pie plate with pastry round, trim and flute edges, and set aside. In a large bowl, toss peaches and cherries in granulated sugar and lemon juice. Let sit for 10 minutes to allow fruit to release their juices. In a small bowl, mix ¼ cup brown sugar, cornstarch, and cinnamon. Add to fruit mixture and toss to coat. Pour filling into pastry and bake for 30 minutes.

Meanwhile, prepare Crumb Topping by pulsing flour, oats, ⅔ cup brown sugar, and cinnamon in a food processor several times to mix. Scatter the butter pieces over the top and pulse until it resembles small crumbs. Empty the crumbs into a large bowl and rub them between your fingers until you have large buttery crumbs. Refrigerate until ready to use.

Remove the pie from the oven and reduce the temperature to 375 degrees. Spread the crumbs over the surface of the pie and press down slightly. Return the pie to the oven and continue to bake until the top is brown and the juices bubble thickly at the edge, 35 to 40 minutes. Cool for at least 2 hours before serving.

Note: The unused pie dough can be rolled out, cut into shapes and sprinkled with cinnamon sugar. Bake on a cookie sheet in 400-degree oven for 8 to 12 minutes.

Very Berry Pie

PEAR CRISP PIE

1 recipe Oatmeal Crisp Pastry Dough
  (see page 42)
8 cups peeled, cored, and sliced pears
  (½-inch thick or thicker)
¾ cup granulated sugar
1 tablespoon lemon juice
3 tablespoons cornstarch
2 to 3 tablespoons chopped crystallized
  ginger
1 teaspoon ground cinnamon
½ teaspoon freshly grated nutmeg

Preheat oven to 400 degrees. Line two pie tins with bottom crusts of Oatmeal Crisp Pastry Dough and set aside.

In a large bowl, combine pears, sugar, lemon juice, cornstarch, ginger, cinnamon, and nutmeg. Toss well. Pour half of mixture into each unbaked pie shell. Cover both pies with vented pastry tops. Seal and crimp or flute edges. Brush tops with cream and sprinkle with sugar, if desired. Bake 1 hour, or until top crusts are golden brown. Makes 12 to 16 servings or 2 pies.

RHUBARB PIE

Pastry for a double-crust pie
  (see page 42)
4 cups frozen rhubarb, partially thawed
1¾ cups granulated sugar
¼ cup all-purpose flour
2 tablespoons cornstarch
¼ teaspoon salt
1 egg
1 drop red food coloring

Preheat oven to 350 degrees. Roll out pastry for bottom crust and line pie tin. Roll out pastry for top crust, fold in half, and cut three ½-inch slits through both layers of crust, then set aside. Place rhubarb in medium mixing bowl; let thaw 10 to 15 minutes. Drain off liquid. In a separate bowl, combine sugar, flour, cornstarch, and salt. Beat egg; blend with flour mixture. Add rhubarb and red food coloring and mix well. Pour into unbaked pie shell. Place top crust over filling. Seal and flute edges. Brush top with milk and sprinkle with sugar, if desired. Bake 45 minutes, or until browned. Makes 6 to 8 servings.

Note: Four cups fresh rhubarb may be substituted for frozen rhubarb. Bake at 350 degrees for 50 to 55 minutes.

PUMPKIN PIE

1½ cups canned pumpkin
½ teaspoon ground cinnamon
½ teaspoon nutmeg
¼ teaspoon ground ginger
¼ teaspoon allspice
½ cup granulated sugar
⅓ cup packed brown sugar
1 teaspoon salt
1½ tablespoons cornstarch
2 eggs
1 cup evaporated milk
1 cup water
Pastry for a single-crust pie
   (see page 41)
Whipped cream, for garnishing

Preheat oven to 375 degrees. Place pumpkin in a large mixing bowl. In a separate bowl, mix cinnamon, nutmeg, ginger, allspice, granulated sugar, brown sugar, salt, and cornstarch. Add to pumpkin and mix until blended. Add eggs and evaporated milk and mix until blended. Add water and mix well. Pour into unbaked pie shell and bake 50 to 60 minutes, or until knife inserted near center comes out clean. Cool on a wire rack. Top with whipped cream before serving. Makes 6 to 8 servings.

PUMPKIN CREAM CHEESE PIE

1 (8-ounce) package cream cheese,
   softened
¾ cup granulated sugar
½ teaspoon salt
1 teaspoon ground cinnamon
½ teaspoon nutmeg
½ teaspoon ground cloves
½ teaspoon ground ginger
2 eggs
1 (16-ounce) can pumpkin
1 teaspoon vanilla
½ cup pecan halves (optional)
1 unbaked 9-inch pie shell

Preheat oven to 350 degrees. In a large bowl, beat cream cheese, sugar, salt, and spices until fluffy. Add eggs, one at a time, beating well after each. Beat in pumpkin and vanilla. Pour into pie shell. Bake 55 minutes, or until knife inserted near center comes out clean. During last 15 minutes of baking, place pecan halves around edges for decoration. Cool on a wire rack, then chill in the refrigerator for 3 to 4 hours. Serve with a dollop of whipped cream and a sprinkle of ground nutmeg. Makes 6 to 8 servings.

BAKED ALASKA PIE

1 9-inch baked pie shell (see page 41)

1 quart peppermint ice cream, slightly
    softened

2 to 3 tablespoons chocolate syrup

5 egg whites

1 teaspoon vanilla

½ teaspoon cream of tartar

⅔ cup sugar

Spoon ice cream into baked pie shell. Drizzle with chocolate syrup. Place in freezer until ready to use.

Heat oven to 500 degrees. With an electric mixer, beat egg whites, vanilla, and cream of tartar until foamy. Gradually beat in sugar until mixture is stiff and glossy. Completely cover ice cream in pie shell with meringue, sealing well to edge of crust and piling high. (If desired, pie may be frozen up to 24 hours at this point.) When ready to serve, bake pie on lowest oven rack for 3 to 5 minutes, or until meringue is light brown. Serve immediately, or return to freezer until ready to serve. Makes 6 to 8 servings.

CHOCOLATE CHIP WALNUT PIE

2 eggs

½ cup pastry flour

⅓ cup granulated sugar

⅓ cup packed dark brown sugar

¾ cup butter, melted and cooled

1 cup semi-sweet chocolate chips

1 cup chopped walnuts

1 9-inch unbaked pie shell (see page 41)

Preheat oven to 350 degrees. Beat eggs with an electric mixer until foamy. Add flour and sugars and mix well. Stir in cooled melted butter. Fold in chocolate chips and walnuts. Pour into unbaked pie shell.

Bake 45 minutes until golden brown and set in the middle. Cool on a wire rack. Serve warm. Makes 6 to 8 servings.

Baked Alaska Pie

HURRAY FOR THE PUMPKIN PIE

First Layer:

⅔ cup milk chocolate chips

1 cup granulated sugar

2 tablespoons butter or margarine

½ cup light corn syrup

¾ teaspoon vanilla

½ cup evaporated milk

¾ cup chopped macadamia nuts

1 10-inch unbaked pie shell

Second Layer:

1 (8-ounce) package cream cheese,
    softened

¼ cup granulated sugar

½ teaspoon vanilla

1 egg, beaten

Third Layer:

1 (15-ounce) can pumpkin

¼ teaspoon salt

1½ cups melted vanilla ice cream

1¼ teaspoons ground cinnamon

3 eggs, beaten

½ teaspoon ground ginger

⅓ cup packed brown sugar

½ teaspoon nutmeg

⅓ cup granulated sugar

¼ teaspoon ground cloves

Topping:

½ cup whipping cream

1 tablespoon powdered sugar

1 (8-ounce) package cream cheese,
    softened

1 cup sugar

¼ cup milk chocolate chips

1 tablespoon margarine

⅓ cup crushed macadamia nuts

Line pie tin with pastry; trim and flute edges. Set aside while preparing first layer.

For first layer: Place milk chocolate chips in a small bowl and set aside. In a heavy saucepan, over medium heat, cook the 1 cup sugar, 2 tablespoons butter, corn syrup, evaporated milk, and ¾ teaspoon vanilla. Bring to a boil and stir continuously for 6 minutes. Remove from heat. Pour ⅓ cup plus 1 tablespoon of this hot caramel mixture over chocolate chips. Stir until smooth. Pour into bottom of pastry-lined pie tin; pat down with back of spoon. Stir macadamia nuts into remaining caramel mixture and allow to cool slightly before spreading over the chocolate.

To prepare second layer: Beat cream cheese with an electric mixer on medium speed until smooth. Beat in the ¼ cup sugar. Add ½ teaspoon vanilla and the beaten egg and beat until light and smooth. Chill for 20 minutes then spread over first layer.

Preheat oven to 450 degrees while preparing third layer. For third layer: Combine pumpkin, salt, melted ice cream, cinnamon, beaten eggs, ginger, brown sugar, nutmeg, the ⅓ cup sugar, and ground cloves in a medium bowl and mix thoroughly. Pour over second layer. Bake 15 minutes at 450 degrees. Reduce heat to 350 degrees and bake 50 minutes. Remove from oven and cool on a wire rack.

Once pie has cooled, prepare topping by beating together whipping cream and powdered sugar until stiff, then set aside. In another bowl, cream the 1 cup sugar and cream cheese until smooth and fluffy. Fold in the whipped cream. With a cookie scoop, dollop topping around edges.

Melt the ¼ cup milk chocolate chips with 1 tablespoon margarine in the microwave on high power in 30-second increments, stirring after each time, until mixture is melted. Cool slightly then drizzle chocolate over the pie and whipped topping. Sprinkle with crushed macadamia nuts. Makes 6 to 8 servings.

Mini Pecan Pies

White Chocolate Macadamia Pie

Mini Pecan Pies

1 recipe Pastry for Double-Crust Pie
    (see page 42)
⅔ cup chopped pecans, divided
1 cup packed brown sugar
⅔ cup light corn syrup
2 teaspoons vanilla
¾ teaspoon salt
2 eggs
2 egg whites

Preheat oven to 375 degrees. Coat muffin tins for 24 muffins with nonstick cooking spray. Roll out pastry dough into a large rectangle. Use a round cookie cutter to cut out large circles. Press a dough circle into each muffin cup, lining the sides and bottom with dough. Divide half of the chopped pecans between the pastry-lined muffin cups; set aside.

In a large bowl, stir remaining ⅓ cup pecans, brown sugar, corn syrup, vanilla, salt, eggs, and egg whites until well combined. Spoon filling into muffin tins. Bake for 20 minutes. Cool in pan 10 minutes, then run knife around the pie crust to loosen. Carefully remove to cooling racks. Serve with vanilla ice cream or whipped cream. Makes 24 mini pies.

White Chocolate Macadamia Pie

1 baked 9-inch pie shell (see page 41)
Filling:
1 (8-ounce) package cream cheese,
    softened
⅓ cup granulated sugar
⅓ cup heavy cream
6.5 ounces white baking chocolate,
    melted
½ teaspoon orange zest
⅔ cup chopped macadamia nuts, roasted
Ganache:
¾ cup semi-sweet chocolate chips
½ cup heavy cream
Topping:
3 cups sweetened whipped cream
1 to 2 tablespoons chopped macadamia
    nuts

Prepare pie filling: Beat cream cheese and sugar with an electric mixer until smooth. Scrape bowl with a spatula and mix in ⅓ cup heavy cream. Add melted white chocolate, orange zest, and nuts and stir just until incorporated. Fold in the whipped cream. Spread into baked pie shell and level off with a rubber spatula. Freeze until solid, about 4 hours.

Thirty minutes to an hour before serving, prepare ganache: Place chocolate chips in a metal mixing bowl and set aside. Bring cream to a simmer over medium heat. Pour simmering cream over chocolate chips and stir until melted. Set aside and allow to cool slightly.

To finish pie, spread warm ganache over top of the frozen pie, smoothing to the edges with a spatula.

For garnish, place sweetened whipped cream in a piping bag and pipe edges of pie with whipped cream. Sprinkle macadamia nuts over top. Refrigerate until ready to serve. Makes 6 to 8 servings.

Note: If desired, you can prepare ganache ahead of time, then reheat before finishing pie. To reheat, place the ganache in the microwave on low power for no more than 10 seconds at a time. Stir after each warming, until ganache pours loosely but is not close to boiling. Be very careful when warming chocolate, as it will burn very quickly when heated in the microwave. Once chocolate is scorched it is unusable.

HARVEST APPLE CRISP

10 cups sliced apples (peeled)
1 cup granulated sugar
1 cup plus 1 tablespoon all-purpose flour
1 teaspoon ground cinnamon
½ cup water
1 cup quick-cooking rolled oats
1 cup packed brown sugar
¼ teaspoon baking powder
¼ teaspoon baking soda
½ cup butter, melted

Preheat oven to 350 degrees. Place the sliced apples in a 9 x 13-inch pan. Mix the granulated sugar, 1 tablespoon of the flour, and the ground cinnamon together, and sprinkle over apples. Pour water evenly over all; set aside. In a large bowl, combine the oats, remaining 1 cup flour, brown sugar, baking powder, baking soda, and melted butter. Stir to combine then crumble evenly over the apple mixture. Bake for about 45 minutes, until top is golden brown and apples are tender.

PEAR AND CHERRY CRISP

1 (16-ounce) package frozen unsweet-
    ened pitted tart red cherries, thawed
    and drained (set juice aside), or 1
    (16-ounce) can pitted tart red cher-
    ries (water packed)
⅓ to ½ cup granulated sugar
2 tablespoons all-purpose flour
1 teaspoon orange zest
½ teaspoon ground cinnamon
3 to 4 medium pears, peeled, cored, and
    thinly sliced (3 cups total)
½ cup granola or streusel
2 tablespoons butter, melted
Vanilla ice cream (optional)

Preheat oven to 375 degrees. If using canned cherries, drain cherries, reserving ½ cup of the juice. In a large mixing bowl, combine frozen or canned cherries and reserved juice; add sugar and toss to coat. Let stand for 5 minutes.

In a small bowl, combine flour, orange zest, and cinnamon. Sprinkle over cherries and toss to mix. Add sliced pears and toss to mix. Transfer mixture to an ungreased 2-quart square baking dish. Combine granola and butter and sprinkle over filling. Bake about 30 minutes, or until pears are tender. If necessary, to prevent overbrowning, cover with foil the last 5 to 10 minutes. Serve warm with ice cream. Serves 8.

Note: Canned, sliced pears can be used in place of fresh pears, if desired.

Harvest Apple Crisp

Polar Bear Claw Cookies and Pumpkin Haystacks

COOKIES AND BARS

CHOCOLATE CHIP COOKIES

1¾ cups (3½ sticks) butter, softened
1¾ cups packed brown sugar
1¼ cups granulated sugar
4 eggs
5½ tablespoons water
1½ teaspoons vanilla
6 cups all-purpose flour
1½ teaspoons salt
1½ teaspoons baking soda
3 cups chocolate chips

Preheat oven to 350 degrees. Line cookie sheets with parchment paper or lightly grease pans and set aside. In a large mixing bowl, cream together butter and sugars. Add eggs, water, and vanilla; mix until creamy. Add flour, salt, and baking soda; mix well. Gently fold in chocolate chips, mixing only until chips are evenly distributed. (Overmixing results in broken chips and discolored dough.) Drop by spoonfuls onto prepared cookie sheets. Bake 8 to 10 minutes, or until golden brown. Makes 5 to 6 dozen 3½-inch cookies.

PUMPKIN HAYSTACKS

4 cups all-purpose flour
2 cups old-fashioned rolled oats
2 teaspoons baking soda
2 teaspoons ground cinnamon
Dash nutmeg
1 teaspoon salt
1½ cups butter, softened
2 cups packed brown sugar
1 cup granulated sugar
1 egg
1 teaspoon vanilla
1 (16-ounce) can solid pack pumpkin
2 cups semi-sweet chocolate chips
1½ cups flaked coconut
1½ cups chopped walnuts

Preheat oven to 350 degrees. In a large bowl, whisk together flour, oats, baking soda, cinnamon, nutmeg, and salt and set aside. Cream together butter and sugars until fluffy. Add egg and vanilla and mix well. Add pumpkin, then gradually add the dry ingredients. Fold in chocolate chips, coconut, and nuts. Scoop batter by spoonfuls onto lightly greased cookie sheets and bake 15 to 20 minutes, or until cookies are firm and lightly browned. Cool on wire racks. Makes 4 dozen cookies.

CHOCOLATE BRICKLE-CHIP COOKIES

1 cup shortening

¾ cup granulated sugar

¾ cup packed brown sugar

2 eggs

1 teaspoon vanilla

1 teaspoon ice cold water

½ teaspoon salt

½ teaspoon baking soda

2 ⅔ cups all-purpose flour

1 (12-ounce) package milk chocolate chips

6 ounces Heath® Bits 'O Brickle Toffee Bits

Preheat oven to 350 degrees. Cream the shortening and sugars together until light and fluffy. Add eggs, vanilla, and ice water. Beat until the mixture is very creamy. Add salt, baking soda, and flour. Mix until incorporated, then add the chocolate chips and toffee bits and stir until fully combined. Refrigerate the dough for at least 1½ hours. Scoop out dough into desired size balls and place on ungreased cookie sheets. Bake until the edges are just turning brown, about 11 minutes. Remove from oven and allow cookies to cool for 3 minutes on cookie sheets. Remove to wire racks to cool. Makes 30 cookies.

CHOCOLATE ORANGE COOKIES

1½ cups all-purpose flour

2 teaspoons baking powder

½ teaspoon salt

1 cup salted butter

2.5 ounces unsweetened baking chocolate, chopped

½ cup packed brown sugar

1 cup granulated sugar

2 teaspoons vanilla

1 teaspoon orange zest

2 eggs

1 cup semi-sweet chocolate chips

1 dark chocolate orange, chopped into 48 ½-inch squares

Dried, sugared orange zest (optional)

Preheat oven to 325 degrees. Whisk together flour, baking powder, and salt in a medium bowl and set aside. Melt butter, baking chocolate, and brown sugar in a small bowl over a pot of simmering water. Stir constantly until all components are completely incorporated; set aside to cool. When chocolate mixture has cooled to room temperature, pour into a large mixing bowl. Add granulated sugar, vanilla, and orange zest. Mix well. Add in eggs until thoroughly mixed. Gradually beat in flour mixture until just combined. Stir in chocolate chips. Drop dough by rounded teaspoonfuls onto ungreased cookie sheets. Press one square of chocolate orange candy into the center of each dough mound. Bake for 12 to 15 minutes, or just until set. Quickly remove to wire racks to cool. Sprinkle with dried, sugared zest, if desired.

For best results, chill dough between batches and only use room temperature cookie sheets. Makes about 4 dozen cookies.

Note: If you can't find a chocolate orange, you can make your own orange chocolate. Melt 1 cup semi-sweet chocolate chips in double boiler or microwave oven. Stir until smooth. Add ½ teaspoon orange extract and stir to combine. Pour out chocolate on a sheet of waxed paper and smooth into a square approximately ¼-inch thick. Place in freezer for about 10 minutes to solidify. Remove from freezer and chop into ½-inch squares.

Cocoa Puffed Chocolate Chip Cookies

2 cups Cocoa Puffs® cereal

2½ cups all-purpose flour

1 teaspoon baking soda

½ teaspoon salt

¾ cup packed light brown sugar

¾ cup granulated sugar

½ cup butter, slightly softened

½ cup butter flavored shortening, chilled

2 eggs

1½ teaspoons vanilla

1½ cups semi-sweet chocolate chips

Preheat oven to 300 degrees. In a blender, blend Cocoa Puffs to small crumbs. Transfer to a medium bowl and whisk in flour, baking soda, and salt and set aside. In a large mixing bowl, blend sugars together, then add butter and shortening and cream well. Add eggs and vanilla and mix at medium speed until just blended. Add the flour mixture and chocolate chips and blend at low speed until just mixed. Using a large ice cream scoop, place on cold, ungreased cookie sheets 2 inches apart. Bake for 18 to 19 minutes, or until just browned. Transfer cookies immediately to a wire rack to cool slightly. For best taste, serve warm from the oven. Makes about 20 cookies.

Oatmeal Cookies

2 cups packed brown sugar

1 cup shortening

2 eggs

½ cup milk

2 cups quick-cooking rolled oats

½ teaspoon salt

1 teaspoon baking soda

½ teaspoon allspice

1 teaspoon ground cinnamon

¼ teaspoon ground cloves

1 teaspoon nutmeg

2 cups all-purpose flour

1 cup raisins

½ cup chopped nuts

Preheat oven to 350 degrees. In a large bowl, cream together sugar and shortening. Add eggs and milk and mix well. Stir in rolled oats. In a separate bowl, sift together salt, baking soda, spices, and flour. Add dry ingredients to wet mixture and mix in until smooth. Stir in raisins and nuts. Drop by rounded teaspoonfuls onto ungreased cookie sheets and bake 10 minutes, or until lightly browned. Makes 3 to 4 dozen cookies.

PEANUT BUTTER BUTTONS

½ cup butter, softened

½ cup peanut butter

½ cup granulated sugar

½ cup packed brown sugar

½ teaspoon baking soda

½ teaspoon baking powder

½ teaspoon vanilla

1 egg

1⅓ cups all-purpose flour

1 (12-ounce) bag miniature peanut
    butter cups (about 36 candies)

½ cup milk chocolate chips

Preheat oven to 350 degrees. In bowl of an electric mixer, cream together butter and peanut butter. Add sugar, brown sugar, baking soda, and baking powder. Beat until combined, making sure all ingredients are incorporated. Beat in vanilla and egg until light and fluffy. Beat in flour just until well combined. Unwrap miniature peanut butter cups. Shape each dough ball around a peanut butter cup until it is completely covered and no chocolate is visible. Place on ungreased baking sheets and bake for 8 minutes. Cookies may look underdone, but do not overbake! Remove from oven and let cookies sit on hot cookie sheets for several more minutes. Transfer cookies to a wire rack to finish cooling. After cookies are completely cooled, melt milk chocolate chips. Drizzle melted chocolate over cooled cookies with a fork or tooth-pick. Allow chocolate to set up. To help the chocolate set up faster, put the cookies in the freezer for a few minutes before drizzling with chocolate. Makes 3 dozen cookies.

SNICKERDOODLES

3 cups granulated sugar, divided

1¼ teaspoons ground cinnamon

1 cup butter, softened

4 eggs

1 teaspoon vanilla

2½ tablespoons water

6 cups all-purpose flour

2 teaspoons cream of tartar

1 teaspoon baking soda

½ teaspoon salt

Preheat oven to 350 degrees. Line cookie sheets with parchment paper. In a medium bowl, mix ½ cup of the sugar and the cinnamon and set aside.

In a large mixing bowl, combine butter and remaining 2½ cups sugar until light and fluffy. Add eggs, vanilla, and water and beat until fluffy. Add flour, cream of tartar, baking soda, and salt, turning mixer on and off in quick bursts at low speed until flour is nearly blended in. Continue mixing at medium speed until well mixed. Shape dough by rounded tablespoonfuls, roll in cinnamon-sugar mixture, then place on prepared cookie sheets. Bake 9 to 10 minutes, or until golden brown. Makes 5 dozen 3-inch cookies.

CHOCOLATE CRACKLE COOKIES

¼ cup shortening, melted

¼ cup cocoa

½ cup vegetable oil

2 cups granulated sugar

4 eggs

2 teaspoons vanilla

2½ cups all-purpose flour

½ teaspoon salt

1½ teaspoons baking powder

½ cup chopped walnuts

½ cup chocolate chips (optional)

½ to 1 cup powdered sugar

Preheat oven to 350 degrees. In a large mixing bowl, cream together shortening, cocoa, oil, sugar, eggs, and vanilla until well mixed. Add flour, salt, and baking powder. Mix well, then add walnuts and chocolate chips, if using. (Dough will be very sticky and almost runny.) Refrigerate dough for 2 to 3 hours or overnight. Place powdered sugar in a shallow bowl. Drop and gently roll dough by tablespoonfuls in powdered sugar, being careful not to overhandle dough. Place on greased or parchment-lined cookie sheets. Bake for 9 to 10 minutes. Do not overbake. The cookie dough may be stored in the refrigerator for up to 5 days; baked cookies will store for at least 2 weeks, if well covered and refrigerated. These cookies freeze beautifully. Makes approximately 5 dozen cookies.

WHITE CHOCOLATE MACADAMIA COOKIES

1 cup butter, softened

1 cup shortening

1½ cups granulated sugar

1½ cups packed brown sugar

1 teaspoon vanilla

4 eggs

4 to 4½ cups all-purpose flour

2 teaspoons salt

2 teaspoons baking soda

1 cup quick-cooking rolled oats

1 cup chopped macadamia nuts

1 (12-ounce) bag white chocolate chips

Preheat oven to 350 degrees. In a large bowl, cream together butter, shortening, and sugars until light and fluffy. Add vanilla. Add eggs, one at a time, mixing after each addition.

In a separate bowl, whisk together flour, salt, baking soda, and oats. Add flour mixture to creamed mixture and blend until incorporated. Fold in nuts and white chocolate chips by hand.

Drop walnut-sized balls of dough onto ungreased cookie sheets and bake 12 to 15 minutes, or until edges are light golden brown. Makes 5 dozen cookies.

Ifs, Ands, and Nuts Cookies

Ifs, Ands, and Nuts Cookies

2 cups flour

2 teaspoons baking soda

1 cup butter

1½ cups brown sugar

½ cup white sugar

1¼ cups peanut butter

2 eggs

1 cup peanuts (unsalted, chopped, and
    roasted a second time)

2½ cups semi-sweet chocolate chips

1 cup peanut butter chips

Preheat oven to 350 degrees. Sift together the flour and soda. Beat butter, sugars, and peanut butter until fluffy. Add eggs and dry ingredients and mix well. Stir in peanuts, chocolate chips, and peanut butter chips. Shape into small balls and place on an ungreased cookie sheet. Flatten with a glass dipped in sugar or make a crisscross with a fork. Bake for 8 to 10 minutes. Makes 2½ dozen cookies.

Polar Bear Claw Cookies

¾ cup white chocolate chips, divided

¾ cup butter, softened

⅔ cup granulated sugar

1 teaspoon vanilla

1 egg

2 cups all-purpose flour

½ teaspoon baking powder

½ teaspoon salt

½ cup cashews

12 caramels, unwrapped

Preheat oven to 375 degrees. Melt half of the white chocolate chips in a large microwave-proof bowl in 20-second increments, stirring until smooth. Add butter to the melted chocolate and beat until creamy. Mix in sugar, vanilla, and egg. Add flour, baking powder, and salt and mix until just blended. Coarsely chop the cashews and caramels. Add nuts, remaining white chocolate chips, and chopped caramels. Place by spoonfuls on greased cookie sheets and bake for 10 to 12 minutes. Makes 30 cookies.

BELLA'S BISCOTTI

½ cup butter

⅔ cup shortening

1 cup packed light brown sugar

1 cup granulated sugar

2 eggs

2 teaspoons vanilla

1¾ cups rolled oats

1¾ cups all-purpose flour

½ teaspoon baking soda

½ teaspoon baking powder

1 teaspoon salt

6 ounces miniature semi-sweet
    chocolate chips

6 ounces butterscotch chips,
    coarsely chopped

¾ cup chopped walnuts

Chocolate glaze:

½ cup cream

½ cup semi-sweet chocolate chips

1 teaspoon vanilla

Preheat oven to 350 degrees. Line a 9 x 13-inch pan with aluminum foil; spray foil with nonstick cooking spray and set aside.

In a large mixing bowl, cream together butter and shortening; add both sugars and mix well. Beat in eggs and vanilla. Grind oats in blender to a fine powder. In a separate bowl, whisk together ground oats, flour, baking soda, baking powder, and salt. Add dry ingredients to wet mixture and beat all together. Stir in mini chips, butterscotch chunks, and nuts. Press dough evenly into foil-lined baking pan. Bake 25 to 30 minutes, or until golden brown and center is set. Cool in pan on wire rack for 30 minutes.

Holding securely to foil lining, gently remove 1 large cookie from pan and place on a cutting board. Leaving cookies on foil lining, cut crosswise into 9 x 1-inch slices. Place slices, cut-side down, 1 inch apart on an un-greased cookie sheet. Bake for 6 to 8 minutes, or until edges are crispy.

Bring cream for chocolate glaze to a boil in a small pan. Add chocolate chips and vanilla. Stir until chips have completely melted, about 3 to 4 minutes. Allow glaze to cool for 10 minutes.

Carefully transfer cookies to a wire rack (cookies will be tender). Cool. Drizzle with chocolate glaze. Let set for several hours. Makes 2 dozen cookies.

Bella's Biscotti

Candy Bar Cookies

CANDY BAR COOKIES

1 box milk chocolate cake mix

½ cup vegetable oil

2 eggs

35 to 40 pieces of your favorite candy bar, such as Rolos®, Junior Mints®, Snickers®, or Milky Way®

Preheat oven to 350 degrees. In a large bowl, mix together dry cake mix, oil, and eggs. Form spoonfuls of dough into balls. Press a piece of candy bar into each dough ball then roll to cover candy bar. Bake on lightly greased cookie sheets for 10 minutes. Makes 35 to 40 cookies.

COCONUT MACAROONS

3 tablespoons light corn syrup

¾ cup plus 2 tablespoons hot water

6 cups desiccated coconut (available at Asian markets)

2 cups granulated sugar

1 teaspoon salt

1½ cups pastry flour

1 egg

1 teaspoon vanilla

Preheat oven to 350 degrees. Grease 2 cookie sheets and set aside.

Add corn syrup to water in a small bowl and set aside. In a medium bowl, mix coconut, sugar, salt, and flour. Add water mixture, egg, and vanilla. Mix on low speed until evenly blended. Allow to rest 30 minutes. Spoon by tablespoonful onto greased cookie sheets. Bake 18 to 20 minutes. Makes 2½ dozen cookies.

CUTOUT SUGAR COOKIES

2 cups granulated sugar

1 cup shortening

3 eggs

1 cup milk

1 teaspoon vanilla

1 teaspoon lemon extract

6½ cups all-purpose flour

1 teaspoon salt

1 teaspoon baking soda

3½ teaspoons baking powder

1 recipe Lemony Buttercream Icing (see below)

Preheat oven to 400 degrees. Line cookie sheets with parchment paper and set aside. In a large mixing bowl, cream together sugar, shortening, and eggs. Add milk, vanilla, and lemon extract and mix at low speed. In a separate bowl, whisk together flour, salt, baking soda, and baking powder. Add to creamed mixture until well blended. Roll out dough ⅛-inch thick; cut into desired shapes and place on prepared baking sheets. Bake 6 minutes, being careful not to overbake. Cookies should be light golden brown around the edges. Cool on wire racks before frosting with Lemony Buttercream Icing. Makes 5 to 6 dozen cookies.

Lemony Buttercream Icing

¾ cup butter, softened

¾ cup shortening

4⅔ cups powdered sugar

1½ teaspoons lemon juice

1½ teaspoons vanilla

⅓ cup water

In a large mixing bowl, combine butter, shortening, and powdered sugar; beat until very creamy. Add lemon juice and vanilla and mix until well blended. Add water and beat until very light, about 2 to 3 minutes.

HAYSTACKS

6 egg whites, lightly beaten

1 cup granulated sugar

3¼ cups flaked coconut

¾ cup chopped dates

½ cup chopped walnuts

¼ teaspoon salt

¾ teaspoon vanilla

Preheat oven to 350 degrees. Combine egg whites and sugar and cook in the top of a double boiler over simmering water until mixture reaches 120 degrees or feels hot to touch. Combine coconut, dates, walnuts, salt, and vanilla in a large mixing bowl. Add hot sugar mixture and blend well. Mixture will be fairly stiff. Using a small ice cream scoop, form into balls and place on lightly greased baking sheets. Bake 20 minutes, or until golden brown. Allow to cool, then remove from pan. Makes 18 cookies.

Cutout Sugar Cookies

CHOCOLATE PRETZEL PASSION COOKIES

1 cup plus 2 tablespoons butter

½ cup plus 2 tablespoons granulated
   sugar

1 cup packed brown sugar

2 eggs

2 tablespoons water

1½ teaspoons vanilla

2½ cups all-purpose flour

¾ teaspoon baking soda

½ teaspoon salt

2 cups broken pretzel pieces

2 cups semi-sweet chocolate chips
   (maxi size)

Preheat oven to 350 degrees. In a large mixing bowl, cream butter until soft. Add sugars and beat until well mixed. Add eggs, water, and vanilla. Beat until fluffy. Add the flour, baking soda, and salt and mix until well incorporated. Add the pretzels and chocolate chips and mix briefly. Scoop with a tablespoon for large cookies or with a teaspoon for smaller cookies and drop onto ungreased cookie sheets. Flatten each dough ball slightly with a glass or the palm of your hand. Bake 10 to 12 minutes. Baking times may vary depending on the size of dough. Makes 30 cookies.

ALMOST OREO COOKIES QUICK & EASY

1 (18-ounce) box devil's food cake mix

2 eggs

3 tablespoons water

3 tablespoons vegetable oil

½ cup cocoa powder

Filling:

1 cup shortening

1 pound plus 1 cup powdered sugar

1 teaspoon vanilla

¼ cup water

Preheat oven to 400 degrees. Combine cake mix, eggs, water, oil, and cocoa powder until well mixed. Form into balls and place on greased cookie sheets. Flatten each ball and bake 6 to 8 minutes. Remove cookies from cookie sheet and place on paper towels. Let cool for 20 to 25 minutes.

Prepare filling: Beat shortening until fluffy. Add 1 cup powdered sugar, vanilla, and water and beat until fluffy. Add half the remaining powdered sugar and beat well. Add remaining powdered sugar and beat well. Place desired amount on one cookie. Place second cookie on top of filling. Gently squeeze together. Repeat until all cookies have been made into sandwiches. Makes 18 cookies.

FROSTED APPLE BITES

¼ cup margarine, softened
1 cup packed brown sugar
1 egg
1 teaspoon baking soda
½ teaspoon salt
¼ teaspoon nutmeg
2 cups all-purpose flour
1 teaspoon vanilla
⅔ cup evaporated milk
1 cup peeled, diced apples
1 cup chocolate chips
1 cup chopped walnuts or pecans
   (optional)
1 recipe Cinnamon Glaze (see below)

Preheat oven to 350 degrees. In a large bowl, cream together margarine, brown sugar, and egg. Add baking soda, salt, nutmeg, and flour. Mix well, then add vanilla and evaporated milk. Fold in apples, chocolate chips, and nuts, if using.

Drop by teaspoonfuls onto greased baking sheets and bake 12 to 14 minutes. Remove cookies to a wire rack. Cool slightly, then frost with Cinnamon Glaze while cookies are still warm. Makes 3 dozen cookies.

Cinnamon Glaze

2 cups powdered sugar
3 tablespoons butter, melted
1 teaspoon ground cinnamon
2 to 3 tablespoons evaporated milk

Mix all ingredients in a medium bowl until smooth and a good consistency for frosting.

PIONEER COOKIES

4 cups whole wheat flour
4 teaspoons baking powder
1 tablespoon ground cinnamon
1 teaspoon allspice
1 cup packed brown sugar
1 cup butter, softened
1 teaspoon vanilla
4 eggs
3 cups finely chopped apples
2 cups raisins

Preheat oven to 350 degrees. Measure flour, baking powder, cinnamon, and allspice into a medium bowl and mix together with a spoon or spatula. Place brown sugar and butter in a large bowl and cream together. Add vanilla and eggs and beat until well mixed and creamy. Stir in the dry ingredients and fold in the apples and raisins. Mix well. Drop by spoonfuls onto greased cookie sheets and bake 10 to 12 minutes. Do not overbake. You can test for doneness by inserting a toothpick. If the toothpick comes out clean the cookies are done. Store in an airtight container. These freeze well. Makes 4 dozen cookies.

Wedding Cookies

WEDDING COOKIES

½ cup granulated sugar
1 cup butter, softened
1 teaspoon vanilla
2 cups all-purpose flour
1 cup chopped walnuts or pecans
Powdered sugar

Preheat oven to 350 degrees. Line cookie sheets with parchment paper and set aside. In a large mixing bowl, cream together sugar, butter, and vanilla. Add flour and mix well. Add nuts and mix. Roll into 1½-inch balls and place on prepared cookie sheets. Bake 10 to 12 minutes. (The tops of cookies should have slight cracks in them and the bottom edges should be just barely light golden brown.) Roll cookies in powdered sugar while very warm. Makes 3 dozen cookies.

ALMOND COOKIES

1 cup butter, softened (no substitutions)
½ cup powdered sugar, plus more for
    dusting baked cookies
1 teaspoon vanilla
½ teaspoon almond extract
1¾ cups all-purpose flour
¾ cup finely chopped almonds
¼ teaspoon salt
1 (8-ounce) can or tube marzipan

Preheat oven to 300 degrees. Line baking sheets with parchment paper and set aside. In a large bowl, cream butter, then gradually beat in powdered sugar. Add vanilla, almond extract, flour, almonds, and salt. Blend well. Chill 1 hour in refrigerator. Roll out dough about ¼-inch thick. Cut out with scalloped cutter (about 2 inches in size) and place on prepared cookie sheets. Sprinkle counter with powdered sugar and roll marzipan out to ¼- inch thick. Cut out ¾-inch circles and press one in the center of each cookie. Bake 15 minutes, until set but not browned. Remove from oven and dust with powdered sugar. Cool. Store in an airtight container. Makes 18 cookies.

PICNIC BROWNIES

4 ounces unsweetened baking chocolate

1 cup butter

2 cups granulated sugar

2 teaspoons vanilla

1 teaspoon salt

4 eggs

1¾ cups all-purpose flour

⅔ cup chopped walnuts, pecans, or almonds

1 cup chocolate chips

Preheat oven to 350 degrees. Grease two 9-inch round pans.

In top of a double boiler or a microwave-safe bowl, melt chocolate and butter. In a medium bowl, mix sugar, vanilla, and salt; add to melted chocolate mixture and blend well. Add eggs, one at a time, beating well after each addition. Add flour and mix well. Divide batter equally into prepared pans. Spread evenly and sprinkle top of each with chopped nuts and chocolate chips. Bake 20 to 25 minutes. Brownies are done when a toothpick inserted an inch from center comes out clean. (Do not overbake.) Allow to cool completely before cutting. Run a thin knife between pan and brownies and turn upside down. With knife that is longer than brownies are wide, cut brownies by pressing knife straight down through brownies; cut each round into 8 wedges. Makes 16 brownies. These brownies store and stack well, for easy portability.

CREAM CHEESE BROWNIES

1 package deluxe brownie mix

1 (8-ounce) package cream cheese, softened

⅓ cup granulated sugar

1 egg

2 tablespoons milk

Follow package directions for preheating oven and preparing cake-like brownies. Pour batter into a greased 9 x 9-inch pan. In a separate bowl, beat cream cheese and sugar until creamy. Add egg and milk and mix until smooth. Drop cream cheese batter into the brownie pan in spoonfuls and swirl with a knife. Bake for 35 to 40 minutes. Cut into 3-inch squares or size desired. Makes 9 to 15 bars.

Variation: For Raspberry Cream Cheese Brownies, dollop approximately ½ cup raspberry jam by spoonfuls on top of cream cheese before swirling.

Picnic Brownies

Pecan Bars, Cream Cheese Brownies, and Lemon Bars

CHEWY CARAMEL BROWNIES

1 package German chocolate cake mix
⅔ cup evaporated milk, divided
1 cup butter, melted
35 caramels, unwrapped
1 cup chocolate chips
1 cup chopped nuts (optional)

Preheat oven to 350 degrees. Grease a 9 x 13-inch cake pan and set aside.

In a large bowl, blend dry cake mix, ⅓ cup of the evaporated milk, and the melted butter until all ingredients are incorporated. Spread two-thirds of this mixture into the prepared pan and bake 7 minutes. Remove from oven to cool.

Melt caramels and remaining evaporated milk in a medium saucepan over medium heat. Pour caramel mixture over the cooled brownies. Sprinkle chocolate chips and nuts (if using) over caramel. Drop small spoonfuls of the remaining brownie batter over top of chocolate chips. Return to the oven and bake an additional 16 to 18 minutes. Makes 2 dozen brownies.

PECAN BARS

Topping:
1½ cups butter
1½ cups packed brown sugar
1½ cups honey
½ cup heavy cream
4 cups pecan halves

Crust:
1 cup butter, softened
1 cup granulated sugar
3 eggs
Grated rind of 1 lemon
4 cups all-purpose flour
½ teaspoon baking powder

Make the topping first and allow it to cool while preparing and baking the crust. To make the topping: Combine butter, sugar, and honey in a saucepan over medium heat. Bring to a boil and cook until it has boiled 5 minutes, stirring constantly. Remove from heat. Cool slightly and stir in cream and pecans.

To make crust: Preheat oven to 375 degrees. Grease a 15 x 10-inch pan. In a large mixing bowl, cream together butter and sugar. Add eggs and lemon rind and beat until smooth. Add flour and baking powder and mix well. Press the dough into the bottom of the pan, pricking evenly with a fork. Bake 12 to 15 minutes, or until dough looks half done. (Overbaking at this point will cause the crust to be too hard by the time the second baking is complete.) Reduce heat to 350. Remove crust from oven and spread topping evenly over the partially baked crust. Return to oven and bake for an additional 30 to 35 minutes, or until topping is set. Cut into bars. Makes about 15 to 24 bars, depending on size.

CHERRY ALMOND SQUARES

1 cup sour cream
¼ cup water
3 eggs
1 box sour cream cake mix
1 can cherry pie filling
¼ cup sliced almonds
1½ cups powdered sugar
2 tablespoons milk

Preheat oven to 350 degrees. Grease and flour a 15½x10½-inch jelly roll pan. Mix sour cream, water, and eggs in a large bowl. Stir in dry cake mix until moistened. Batter will be slightly lumpy. Spread into prepared pan. Drop pie filling by generous spoonfuls onto batter. Bake 25 to 30 minutes or until cake springs back when touched lightly. Cool. In a small bowl, combine powdered sugar and milk, stirring until a smooth glaze forms. Drizzle glaze over top. Sprinkle with almonds. Cut into bars. Makes 3 dozen bars.

CARAMEL-ALMOND DREAM BARS

35 caramels, unwrapped
1 (15-ounce) can sweetened condensed
    milk
1 cup butter, softened
1⅓ cups packed brown sugar
2 teaspoons vanilla
½ teaspoon almond extract
½ teaspoon baking soda
1 cup all-purpose flour
3 cups rolled oats
1 cup slivered almonds
Whole almonds, for garnishing

Preheat oven to 350 degrees. Melt caramels and half of the sweetened condensed milk together in a medium saucepan over low heat. While caramels are melting, cream together butter, brown sugar, vanilla, and almond extract in a large bowl. Add baking soda, flour, and oats. Press half of the mixture into a greased 11 x 7-inch pan. Pour melted caramels over the top and spread almost to edge. Stir 1 cup almonds into last half of oatmeal mixture and spread on top. Place 1 whole almond on top of mixture every 1 to 2 inches; drizzle condensed milk over top of pan. Bake for 30 minutes. Cool on a wire rack, then cut into squares. Makes 2 dozen bars.

NO-BAKE CARAMEL COOKIES

2 cups granulated sugar
¾ cup butter
⅔ cup evaporated milk
1 (4-ounce) package instant butterscotch
    pudding mix
3½ cups quick-cooking rolled oats

In a large saucepan, combine sugar, butter, and evaporated milk. Bring to a rolling boil, stirring frequently. Remove from heat and add butterscotch pudding mix and oatmeal; mix together thoroughly. Cool 15 minutes. Drop by spoonfuls onto waxed paper. Allow cookies 15 minutes to set. Makes 5 dozen cookies.

Cherry Almond Squares

Hu La La Surprise Cookies

2½ cups all-purpose flour

1 cup sugar

1 cup brown sugar

1 teaspoon baking powder

¾ teaspoon baking soda

¾ teaspoon salt

1 cup butter

2 cups coconut

2 cups rolled oats

3 eggs

1 teaspoon vanilla

2 cups milk chocolate chips

Preheat oven to 350 degrees. In a medium mixing bowl, combine flour, sugars, baking powder, baking soda, and salt. Cut in butter and mix until well blended. Add coconut and oatmeal and mix briefly. Add eggs and vanilla. Mix well. Stir in chocolate chips.

Bake 10 to 12 minutes. Makes 3½ dozen cookies.

Lemon Bars

½ cup butter, softened

¼ cup powdered sugar, plus more for
    dusting top

1⅛ cups all-purpose flour

2 eggs

1 cup granulated sugar

2 tablespoons lemon juice

Grated rind of half a lemon

Preheat oven to 325 degrees. In a large bowl, cream butter and powdered sugar. Mix in 1 cup of the flour. Spread in an 8 x 8-inch pan and bake 15 to 20 minutes. While crust is baking, prepare the lemon layer. Beat eggs slightly. Add sugar, remaining flour, lemon juice, and rind. Mix well and pour over hot crust. Bake an additional 18 to 22 minutes, or until the center is set. Remove from oven and sprinkle with sifted powdered sugar. Cool slightly before cutting into bars. Makes 1 dozen bars.

Note: This recipe may be doubled and baked in a 9 x 13-inch pan.

OATMEAL FUDGE BARS

1 cup butter or margarine, softened
2 cups packed brown sugar
2 eggs
2 teaspoons vanilla
2½ cups all-purpose flour
1 teaspoon baking soda
½ teaspoon salt
1½ cups quick-cooking rolled oats
1 (14-ounce) can sweetened condensed
    milk
1 (12-ounce) package semi-sweet
    chocolate chips
¼ cup margarine
2 teaspoons vanilla
1 cup chopped walnuts (optional)

Preheat oven to 350 degrees. Grease a 9x13-inch baking pan and set aside. In a large mixing bowl, cream together butter and brown sugar; add eggs and vanilla. In a small bowl, sift flour, baking soda, and salt and add to creamed mixture. Mix in oats. In heavy saucepan, mix sweetened condensed milk, chocolate chips, and margarine and heat until chocolate is just melted. Stir in vanilla and nuts.

Spread two-thirds of the dough into prepared baking pan. Spread with chocolate mixture. Drop remaining one-third of dough on top by spoonfuls. Bake for 25 minutes. Cool, then cut into bars. Makes 36 bars.

HEAVENLY COOKIE BARS

¾ cup butter, softened
¾ cup granulated sugar
¾ cup packed brown sugar
3 tablespoons water
1½ teaspoons vanilla
1 egg
1½ cups all-purpose flour
1½ teaspoons baking powder
1 teaspoon salt
1½ cups chocolate chips
1½ cups flaked coconut
1 cup chopped nuts (optional)

Preheat oven to 300 degrees. Lightly grease a 9 x 13-inch pan and set aside. In a large bowl, beat butter until smooth. Add sugars and cream well. Mix in water, vanilla, and eggs. Stir in flour, baking powder, and salt and mix well. Add chocolate chips, coconut, and nuts. Mix together and spread evenly in prepared pan. Bake for 25 to 30 minutes. Allow to cool, then cut into squares. Makes 2 dozen squares.

Cookie Brittle

COOKIE BRITTLE

1 cup butter or margarine, softened
1½ teaspoons vanilla
½ teaspoon salt
1 cup granulated sugar
2 cups all-purpose flour
1 (6-ounce) package chocolate chips or
    butterscotch chips
1 cup walnuts, chopped

Preheat oven to 375 degrees. Cream butter, vanilla, and salt in a large bowl. Gradually beat in sugar; add flour, chocolate chips, and ¾ cup of the walnuts. Mix well and press evenly into an ungreased 10 x 15-inch jelly roll pan. Sprinkle remaining nuts over top and press lightly. Bake 25 minutes, or until golden brown. Cool and break in irregular pieces to serve.

NO-BAKE CHOCOLATE BARS

½ cup granulated sugar
½ cup light corn syrup
1 cup chunky peanut butter
1 teaspoon vanilla
3 cups Corn Flakes® cereal, crushed
¾ cup chocolate chips

Warm sugar, corn syrup, peanut butter, and vanilla in a medium saucepan; do not cook. Once mixture is warm and combined, add Corn Flakes (measured before being crushed). Stir together and spread in a 9 x 9-inch pan. Melt chocolate chips and spread on top. Makes 16 bars.

CHEWY BUTTERSCOTCH CRISPY BARS

1 cup granulated sugar
1¼ cups light corn syrup
1½ cups creamy peanut butter
5½ cups Rice Krispies® cereal
1 (12-ounce) package butterscotch chips
1 (12-ounce) package semi-sweet choco-
    late chips

Butter a 9 x 13-inch glass pan and set aside. Place sugar and corn syrup in a large pan and bring to a boil, stirring constantly. Stir in peanut butter until smooth; remove from heat. Stir in cereal until well coated. Spread mixture into the buttered pan and set aside.

Place butterscotch chips in a nonstick saucepan. Melt over low to medium heat, stirring constantly. Add chocolate chips; stir until well blended and completely melted. Spread over cereal mixture. When firm, cut into squares. Makes 20 squares.

Chiffon Cake

CAKES

CHIFFON CAKE

1¼ cups granulated sugar
1 tablespoon baking powder
2¼ cups cake flour
1 teaspoon salt
½ cup salad or vegetable oil
5 egg yolks
¾ cup water
2 teaspoons vanilla
1 cup (7 to 8 large) egg whites
½ teaspoon cream of tartar
2 (23-ounce) cans lemon pie filling
1 (8-ounce) carton nondairy whipped
    topping

Preheat oven to 325 degrees. Sift dry ingredients together in a large bowl. Add oil, egg yolks, water, and vanilla and mix until smooth, then set aside. In a separate, clean bowl with clean beaters, whip egg whites with cream of tartar until stiff. Pour batter over whipped whites, folding together until blended. Bake in an ungreased 10-inch tube pan for 55 minutes. To test doneness, lightly press finger on the cake. It will spring back when done. Invert tube pan and let hang until cool.

Once cake is cool, slice horizontally into 3 layers. Separate layers. Spread a thin layer (about half of a can) of lemon pie filling on cut side of bottom layer, then place the next layer on top of the pie filling and spread the top of that layer with pie filling. Replace cake top. In a small bowl, fold three-quarters of a can of pie filling into the whipped topping and frost inside the hole, outside the cake, and on top of the cake. Store cake in refrigerator. Makes 14 servings.

DUMP CAKE QUICK & EASY

1 (26-ounce) can cherry pie filling
1 (20-ounce) can crushed pineapple
1 package yellow or white cake mix
¾ cup butter

Preheat oven to 350 degrees. Grease a 9 x 13-inch cake pan. Dump pie filling in the bottom of pan and spread as evenly as possible. Dump crushed pineapple, with juice, evenly over pie filling. Sprinkle cake mix evenly over the fruit. Do not stir. Slice butter thinly and place slices over cake mix. Try to cover mix. Bake 45 minutes. Serve with a dollop of whipped cream or a scoop of vanilla ice cream.

CARROT CAKE

2 cups all-purpose flour

1 teaspoon salt

1 teaspoon baking soda

2 teaspoons ground cinnamon

½ cup coconut

½ cup walnuts

½ cup raisins

2 cups granulated sugar

1 cup vegetable oil

4 eggs

3 cups peeled and grated carrots

1 recipe Cream Cheese Icing (below)

Preheat oven to 350 degrees. Lightly grease and flour two 9-inch round or square cake pans or a 9 x 13-inch pan and set aside.

Whisk together flour, salt, baking soda, and cinnamon in a large bowl and set aside. Combine coconut, walnuts, and raisins in a food processor or blender and process until very fine (or chop with knife until very, very fine). In a large mixing bowl, combine sugar and oil and mix well. Add eggs, one at a time, beating until creamy. Add dry ingredients and mix until well blended. Add ground nut mixture and grated carrots and beat until blended. Divide batter equally into pans and bake 40 to 45 minutes. Allow to cool 10 minutes before removing from pans and placing on cooling racks. When completely cool, frost with Cream Cheese Icing. Makes 12 servings.

Cream Cheese Icing QUICK & EASY

2 (8-ounce) packages cream cheese, softened

½ cup butter, at room temperature

5 cups powdered sugar

2 teaspoons vanilla

Beat cream cheese until softened. Add butter and mix until blended. Add 3 cups powdered sugar and beat until blended. Add remaining powdered sugar and vanilla and beat until smooth and fluffy. Do not overmix, or icing will be runny.

TOFFEE TORTE QUICK & EASY

1 package devil's food cake mix

1 (16-ounce) carton frozen whipped topping, thawed

7 English toffee bars (Heath® or Skor®), crushed

Grease and flour two 9-inch round cake pans. Prepare and bake the cake according to package directions. Cool on a wire rack. (If time permits the cakes can be frozen for easier handling.) Carefully cut each layer in half horizontally. Place thawed whipped topping in a bowl and fold in 6 of the crushed candy bars. Place one layer of the cake on a serving plate and spread with ½ cup of the topping mixture. Repeat with the remaining 3 layers. Frost the sides and top with the topping mixture. Sprinkle the remaining crushed bar on top of the cake.

Note: If desired, you can substitute a double recipe of Stabilized Whipped Cream (recipe on page 103) for the frozen whipped topping.

Carrot Cake

PEPPERMINT TORTE

QUICK
& EASY

1 package devil's food cake mix

¼ cup finely crushed peppermint
   candies

½ (10.5-ounce) bag miniature
   marshmallows

1 cup chopped walnuts—optional

2 (12-ounce) cartons frozen nondairy
   whipped topping, thawed

15 to 20 starlight mints

½ (1 pound) package chocolate sandwich
   cookies, crushed

Prepare devil's food cake mix according to package directions and bake in two greased and floured 9-inch round cake pans. Turn out of pans and allow to cool on wire racks. When cakes are cool, slice each layer in half horizontally to make 4 thin layers. Place a piece of waxed paper between each layer and put sliced cake in the freezer while you make the filling.

To make filling, combine peppermint candies, marshmallows, nuts, and 1 container of the whipped topping. Mix until smooth. Chill, covered, in refrigerator 2 to 3 hours. Remove cake layers from the freezer and separate. Spread one-third of the peppermint filling on the first layer and then place another layer of cake on top of the filling. Repeat this process with the next 2 layers. Place the last layer on top and frost the sides and top with the second container of whipped topping. Take a handful of cookie crumbs and gently pat on to the side of cake. Repeat until sides of cake are covered with crumbs. Garnish with rosettes of whipped topping, starlight mints, and cookie crumbs. Makes 14 to 16 servings.

OATMEAL CAKE

1½ cups boiling water

1 cup rolled oats

½ cup shortening

1 cup packed brown sugar

1 cup granulated sugar

2 eggs, well beaten

1½ cups all-purpose flour

1 teaspoon ground cinnamon

½ teaspoon nutmeg

1 teaspoon baking soda

½ teaspoon salt

Topping:

½ cup butter

1 cup packed brown sugar

⅓ cup evaporated milk

1 cup flaked coconut

1 cup chopped nuts

1 teaspoon vanilla

Preheat oven to 350 degrees. Grease and flour a broiler-safe 9 x 13-inch baking pan and set aside. Pour boiling water over oats and let stand until cool. In a large bowl, cream together shortening, sugars, and eggs until fluffy. Add oats and water mixture and stir to combine. Sift together flour, cinnamon, nutmeg, baking soda, and salt and blend into creamed mixture. Pour batter into prepared pan and bake 35 to 45 minutes, or until cake tests done when a toothpick inserted near center comes out clean.

Prepare topping while cake is baking: Melt butter in microwave in a medium bowl. Blend in sugar. Add remaining ingredients and spread over cake as soon as it is removed it from oven. Place cake under broiler for 1 to 2 minutes to caramelize the topping. Serves 12 to 15.

RAVE REVIEWS COCONUT CAKE   QUICK & EASY

Cake:

1 package yellow cake mix

1 (3-ounce) package instant vanilla
    pudding mix

1 ⅓ cups water

4 eggs

¼ cup vegetable oil

2 cups flaked coconut

1 cup chopped walnuts or pecans

Cream Cheese Filling:

4 tablespoons butter

2 cups flaked coconut

1 (8-ounce) package cream cheese,
    softened

2 teaspoons milk

3½ cups sifted powdered sugar

½ teaspoon vanilla

Preheat oven to 350 degrees. Grease and flour three 9-inch round cake pans and set aside.

Prepare cake: Blend cake mix, pudding mix, water, oil, and eggs in a large bowl. Using an electric mixer, beat 4 minutes at medium speed. Stir in coconut and nuts. Pour into prepared pans and bake 30 to 35 minutes. Cool in pans for 15 minutes, then turn out onto wire racks.

When cakes are cool, prepare Cream Cheese Filling: Melt 2 tablespoons of the butter in a large skillet over low heat. Add coconut, stirring constantly, until golden brown. Spread coconut out on absorbent paper to cool and drain off excess butter. Cream remaining butter with cream cheese. Add milk and gradually beat in sugar and vanilla. Stir in 1¾ cups of the toasted coconut.

Place bottom cake layer on serving plate and top with a generous mound of frosting. Spread frosting to within ½ inch of edge of cake. Place second layer on top and repeat, topping with third layer. Frost top of third layer and sides of cake with remaining frosting. Sprinkle remaining toasted coconut on top of cake. This cake is very rich, so small slices are recommended when serving. Makes about 16 servings.

POPPY SEED CAKE

1 (18-ounce) package yellow cake mix

1 (4-ounce) instant vanilla pudding mix

4 eggs

1 cup thick sour cream

½ cup water

1 teaspoon rum flavoring

½ cup butter or margarine, melted

¼ cup poppy seeds

Preheat oven to 350 degrees. Grease and flour a Bundt pan and set aside. In the large bowl of an electric mixer, combine cake and pudding mixes, eggs, sour cream, water, rum flavoring, melted butter, and poppy seeds. Blend well on low speed, then beat at medium speed for 5 minutes. Pour batter into prepared Bundt pan. Bake about 45 minutes, or until cake tests done when a toothpick inserted near center comes out clean. Remove from oven and cool in pan for 15 minutes. Turn out onto cake rack and cool completely. Sift a light dusting of powdered sugar over cake, if desired. Makes 14 servings.

Note: This delicious dessert cake may also be sliced thin and served as a bread with fruit salad.

Sting of the Bee Cake

Bienenstich (Sting of the Bee) Cake

Topping:

½ cup butter (no substitutes)

½ cup granulated sugar

2 tablespoons milk

1 cup slivered almonds

2 teaspoons vanilla

Cake:

1 cup butter (no substitutes)

⅔ cup granulated sugar

2 eggs

3 cups all-purpose flour, sifted

1 tablespoon baking powder

1 teaspoon salt

½ cup milk

Filling:

1 cup butter, softened (no substitutes)

2 cups powdered sugar

2 egg yolks

2 teaspoons vanilla

½ cup raspberry preserves

Prepare topping: In a medium saucepan over medium heat, melt butter until almost boiling. Add sugar and bring to a boil, stirring constantly. Slowly add milk; stir carefully, as mixture will pop. Return to a boil and add almonds. Bring to a boil once again. Remove from heat and stir in vanilla. Allow mixture to cool to room temperature, or, if in a hurry, cool in refrigerator until thick and cool to the touch. For best finished cake, topping should be same temperature as cake batter.

Prepare cake: Preheat oven to 375 degrees. Place a round of parchment paper on the bottom of a 10-inch springform pan. Coat sides of pan with nonstick cooking spray and lightly dust with flour.

With an electric mixer, cream together butter and sugar until soft; add eggs and mix well. Mix in dry ingredients then slowly add milk. Beat until batter is thick and does not stick to the bowl. The batter will be more like a biscuit dough than a traditional cake batter.

Spread batter evenly in springform pan. Sprinkle a small amount of flour on top of batter; gently tap batter down with flat bottom of a cup. (Batter should feel firm and press against the sides of pan.) Pour topping over batter and spread evenly. Cover pan with foil and bake 30 minutes. Remove foil and bake an additional 10 to 15 minutes, or until cake looks firm and golden brown. Allow to cool. Remove pan when completely cooled.

While cake cools, prepare butter-cream filling. Beat butter until soft and creamy. Add powdered sugar, egg yolks, and vanilla and beat until fluffy. Split cake in half horizontally. Spread butter cream filling on bottom of split cake. Spread preserves on top of filling and replace cake top. Makes 16 to 20 servings.

ZUCCHINI PINEAPPLE CAKE

3 eggs

2 cups granulated sugar

2 teaspoons vanilla

1 cup vegetable oil

2 cups grated zucchini

3 cups all-purpose flour

1 teaspoon salt

1 teaspoon baking soda

1 teaspoon baking powder

1 teaspoon ground cinnamon

1 cup crushed pineapple, drained well

½ cup flaked coconut or raisins

1 cup chopped walnuts (optional)

1 recipe Cream Cheese Icing
(see page 94)

Preheat oven to 350 degrees. Grease and flour a 9x13-inch baking pan and set aside.

In a large bowl, combine eggs, sugar, vanilla, and oil and beat mixture until fluffy. Fold in zucchini. Whisk together flour, salt, baking powder, baking soda, and cinnamon then fold into wet batter. Blend in pineapple, coconut, and nuts, if using. Bake 40 to 45 minutes, or until toothpick inserted near center comes out clean. Cool on a wire rack, then frost with Cream Cheese Icing.

YVONI'S PINEAPPLE CAKE

 QUICK
& EASY

1 package yellow (pudding in the mix)
cake mix

½ cup cream of coconut

½ cup pineapple juice

4 eggs

⅓ cup oil

¾ cup crushed pineapple, drained

1 cup sliced fresh strawberries (optional)

1 ½ cups Stabilized Whipped Cream (see
page 103) or nondairy whipped topping, thawed (optional)

Preheat oven to 350 degrees. Grease and flour a 9 x 13-inch cake pan and set aside.

In a large mixing bowl, combine dry cake mix, cream of coconut, pineapple juice, eggs, and oil. Blend well, then fold in ½ cup of the crushed pineapple. Place in prepared pan and bake 40 to 50 minutes; cake is done when a toothpick inserted near center comes out clean. Remove from oven and cool on a wire rack.

If desired, drain remaining crushed pineapple well. Fold pineapple and strawberries into Stabilized Whipped Cream and spread over top of cake. Serves about 15.

Note: Cake may be baked in any shape pan, such as a Bundt pan or an angel food cake pan.

Yvoni's Pineapple Cake

Chocolate Cream Cake

CHOCOLATE CREAM CAKE

1 package devil's food cake mix
1 recipe Stabilized Whipped Cream
  (below)
1 recipe Chocolate Frosting (below)

Prepare and bake cake according to package directions for two 9-inch round layers. Cool and split cake layers horizontally. (Only 3 of the 4 layers are used in this recipe. Freeze extra layer for later use.) While cake is baking, prepare Stabilized Whipped Cream and Chocolate Frosting according to directions below.

To assemble cake: Place one layer of cake on a serving plate. Spoon half of the Stabilized Whipped Cream on cake layer and spread evenly to within half an inch of edge of cake. Place second cake layer on top of cream. Spoon remaining cream on top of layer and again spread evenly to within half an inch of edge of cake. Place third layer on top of cream and gently press down on top layer to set layers together. Frost entire cake with Chocolate Frosting. If desired, garnish with chopped walnuts. Makes 14 to 16 servings.

Stabilized Whipped Cream

1 envelope (1 tablespoon) unflavored
  gelatin
¼ cup cold water
3 cups heavy whipping cream
¾ cup powdered sugar
1½ teaspoons vanilla

In a small saucepan, combine gelatin with water; let stand until gelatin softens, about 5 minutes. Turn heat to low and stir constantly until gelatin is just dissolved. Remove from heat and allow to cool slightly, but do not allow to thicken. In a large mixing bowl, whip cream, sugar, and vanilla until slightly thick. On low speed, gradually add gelatin, then beat on high until cream is thick and peaks hold their shape.

Note: Stabilized Whipped Cream will hold up for 4 to 5 days without separating. It may also be used to garnish cheesecakes or in any recipe calling for whipped cream or nondairy whipped topping.

Chocolate Frosting

4 tablespoons cocoa
3 cups powdered sugar
¼ cup butter or margarine, softened
2 to 3 tablespoons milk
1 teaspoon vanilla

In mixing bowl, whisk together cocoa and powdered sugar. Add softened butter, milk, and vanilla. Beat with an electric mixer until smooth.

SINFULLY DELICIOUS CAKE QUICK & EASY

1 package German chocolate cake mix

1 (15-ounce) can sweetened condensed milk

½ (11-ounce) bottle caramel ice cream topping

1 (12-ounce) carton nondairy frozen whipped topping, thawed

1 Skor® candy bar, crushed

Bake cake mix according to high altitude directions on package. While cake is still hot, poke holes with the end of a wooden spoon or straw over the surface of the cake. Pour condensed milk evenly over holes, followed by caramel topping. Refrigerate cake until time to serve. Before serving, spread whipped topping on top and sprinkle with crushed candy bar. Makes 12 servings.

FUDGE RIBBON CAKE

1 package chocolate cake mix

4 ounces cream cheese, softened

1 tablespoon butter

1 extra small egg

1½ teaspoons cornstarch

1 teaspoon vanilla

½ (15-ounce) can sweetened condensed milk

1 recipe Chocolate Cream Frosting (see below)

Preheat oven to 325 degrees. Grease and flour two 9-inch round cake pans. Prepare cake batter according to package directions and fill prepared pans one-third full. Set aside.

Blend cream cheese and butter in a small mixing bowl until smooth and creamy. In a separate bowl, mix egg, cornstarch, and vanilla; add to cream cheese mixture. Add sweetened condensed milk and beat for one minute. Pour half of cream cheese mixture over cake batter in each pan and bake 45 to 60 minutes, or until cake tests done when a toothpick inserted near center comes out clean. Cool slightly, then turn out cakes onto wire racks and cool completely. Place one layer on serving platter and frost top with Chocolate Cream Frosting. Place second layer on top and frost top and sides of cake. Makes 14 servings.

Chocolate Cream Frosting

¾ cup butter, softened

5 tablespoons shortening

3 tablespoons cocoa

4⅔ cup powdered sugar

1½ teaspoons vanilla

¼ cup plus 1½ teaspoons water

Beat butter, shortening, cocoa, and powdered sugar in a large mixing bowl with an electric mixer until very creamy. Add vanilla and mix until well blended. Add water and mix until very light.

Sinfully Delicious Cake

Cream-Filled Cupcakes

CREAM-FILLED CUPCAKES QUICK & EASY

1 package cake mix, any flavor
1 cup hot water
⅓ cup vegetable oil
4 eggs
⅓ cup all-purpose flour
⅓ cup granulated sugar
1 cup milk
½ cup margarine
½ cup white shortening
¾ cup granulated sugar
1 teaspoon vanilla
Dash salt

Preheat oven to 350 degrees. Line muffin tins with cupcake papers and set aside.

Prepare cupcakes: In a large bowl, beat together cake mix, hot water, vegetable oil, and eggs until well mixed. Fill cupcake papers one-third to one-half full. Bake 13 to 15 minutes. Cool.

While cupcakes cool, combine flour, the ⅓ cup sugar, and milk in a medium saucepan over medium heat. Stir out all lumps. Bring to a boil and cook until thick. Remove from heat, cool mixture, then add margarine, shortening, remaining sugar, vanilla, and salt. Beat with an electric mixer for about 5 minutes until fluffy. Fill a decorating bag that has a no. 4 tip attached. Insert tip into center of the cupcakes and squeeze in a small amount of filling. Ice with remaining cream. Makes 24 to 30 cupcakes.

CHOCOLATE CHERRY CAKE QUICK & EASY

1 package devil's food or chocolate cake mix
1 (26-ounce) can cherry pie filling
2 eggs
1 cup granulated sugar
6 tablespoons butter
⅓ cup milk
1 (12-ounce) package semi-sweet chocolate chips
1 teaspoon vanilla

Preheat oven to 350 degrees. Grease and flour a 9 x 13-inch cake pan. In a large bowl, combine cake mix, cherry pie filling, and eggs. Stir together with large spoon or rubber spatula. (Do not use a mixer; it will break up the cherries.) Spread batter into prepared pan. Bake 30 to 40 minutes, or until cake is set.

While cake is baking, combine sugar, butter, and milk in a large saucepan. Bring to a boil over medium-high heat, and then boil for 1 minute, stirring constantly. Remove from heat and add chocolate chips and vanilla. Stir with a wire whisk until the chips are melted and frosting is smooth. Pour over warm cake and spread to cover. Let cool on wire rack before serving. Makes 16 servings.

CHOCOLATE MACAROON CAKE

Coconut Mixture:

1 egg white (reserve yolk for frosting)

½ cup granulated sugar

1 teaspoon vanilla

1 tablespoon all-purpose flour

2 cups finely grated coconut

Cake Batter:

¾ cup hot water

½ cup cocoa

3 eggs, separated

2 cups granulated sugar, divided

½ cup sour cream

1 teaspoon baking soda

½ cup shortening

1 teaspoon vanilla

1 teaspoon salt

2 cups all-purpose flour

Frosting:

1 cup chocolate chips

2 tablespoons butter

1 egg yolk (reserved from Coconut Mixture)

¼ cup half and half

1¾ cups powdered sugar

Preheat oven to 350 degrees. Grease and flour an angel food cake pan and set aside.

Prepare Coconut Mixture: In a medium bowl, beat egg white until soft mounds form. Add sugar and vanilla, gradually beating until stiff peaks form. In a separate bowl, toss flour and coconut together, then stir slowly into egg white mixture. Set mixture aside.

Prepare Cake Batter: In a small bowl, measure hot water and add cocoa. Stir to dissolve, then set aside. In a large mixing bowl, beat egg whites until soft mounds form; gradually add one half of the sugar, beating until meringue stands in stiff peaks. Set aside. Place sour cream in a medium bowl and fold the baking soda into it. The mixture will grow as you stir it. Set aside. In another bowl, beat remaining sugar, shortening, egg yolks, salt, and vanilla until creamy. Add half of the cocoa mixture and beat until creamy, about 4 minutes. Add the flour, sour cream mixture, and remaining cocoa mixture; blend well. Fold in egg white mixture.

Place one-third of the cake batter in bottom of prepared pan, then crumble half of the coconut mixture on top of batter. Spread half of the remaining cake batter on top of the coconut mixture. Crumble the rest of the coconut mixture on top of the second layer of cake batter, then spread the remaining cake batter on top of the coconut mixture, for a total of 5 layers. Bake for 55 to 65 minutes, or until cake tests done when a toothpick inserted near center comes out clean. Remove from oven and allow to cool until bottom of pan feels slightly warm. To loosen the sides and center, slide a thin knife along the edges and carefully turn pan upside down. Allow to cool completely.

Prepare Frosting: Melt chocolate chips and butter together in a small saucepan. Mix together with egg yolk, half and half, and powdered sugar. Beat until mixture reaches desired spreading consistency. You may need to add a little more half and half to reach proper consistency. Frost cake, slice, and serve. Makes 14 to 16 servings.

Peppermint Cheesecake

½ (1-pound) package of Oreo® cookies

3 (8-ounce) packages cream cheese, softened

1 cup granulated sugar

3 eggs

¾ teaspoon vanilla

1 teaspoon peppermint extract

2 drops red food coloring

2 cups sour cream

3 tablespoons granulated sugar

½ teaspoon vanilla

Peppermint candies, crushed

Preheat oven to 300 degrees. Crush whole Oreo cookies, including frosting centers, to make 2 cups fine crumbs. Press evenly onto bottom of a 10-inch springform pan and set aside.

In a large mixing bowl, beat cream cheese until smooth; gradually add sugar, then add eggs, one at a time, beating well after each addition. Stir in vanilla, peppermint extract, and red food coloring. Pour filling into crust and bake 55 minutes.

When cheesecake is almost finished baking, beat sour cream with a wire whisk; add sugar and vanilla and mix well. Spread on top of cheesecake and return to oven. Bake 10 more minutes. Cool before removing sides from springform pan. Garnish with crushed peppermint candy. Refrigerate until ready to serve. Makes 10 to 12 servings.

Chocolate Cheesecake

½ (1-pound) package of Oreo® cookies

3 (8-ounce) packages cream cheese, softened

1 cup granulated sugar

3 eggs

¾ teaspoon vanilla

⅓ cup chocolate syrup

2 cups sour cream

3 tablespoons granulated sugar

½ teaspoon vanilla

Chocolate chips, for garnishing

Preheat oven to 300 degrees.

Crush whole Oreo cookies, including frosting centers, to make 2 cups of fine crumbs. Press evenly onto bottom and sides of 10-inch springform pan.

In a large mixing bowl, beat cream cheese until smooth; gradually add sugar, then add eggs, one at a time, beating well after each addition. Stir in vanilla and chocolate syrup. Pour filling into crust. Bake 55 minutes.

When cheesecake is almost finished baking, beat sour cream with a wire whisk; add sugar and vanilla and mix well. Spread on top of cheesecake and return to oven. Bake 10 more minutes. Cool before removing sides from springform pan. Garnish with a few chocolate chips. Refrigerate until ready to serve. Makes 10 to 12 servings.

Note: All cheesecakes can be baked, cooled, and frozen for an easy dessert later.

Lion House Cheesecake

LION HOUSE CHEESECAKE

Crust:

1½ cups finely crushed graham cracker
    crumbs

3 tablespoons granulated sugar

6 tablespoons butter, melted

Filling:

3 (8-ounce) packages cream cheese,
    softened

1 cup granulated sugar

2 teaspoons lemon juice

3 eggs

¾ teaspoon vanilla

Topping:

2 cups sour cream

3 tablespoons granulated sugar

½ teaspoon vanilla

Preheat oven to 300 degrees.

Prepare Crust: Thoroughly mix graham cracker crumbs, sugar, and melted butter. Press firmly onto bottom and sides of a 10-inch pie pan or springform pan; set aside while preparing filling.

Filling: In a large mixing bowl, beat cream cheese until smooth; add sugar a little at a time. Add lemon juice. Add eggs, one at a time, beating after each addition. Mix in vanilla and combine thoroughly. Pour into crust; fill to within ½ inch of top to allow room for topping. Bake 55 to 60 minutes, until set (or until the center does not move when the pan is gently moved).

When cheesecake is almost finished baking, beat sour cream with a wire whisk; add sugar and vanilla and mix well. Pour over cake and bake an additional 10 minutes. Cool completely. Refrigerate until ready to serve. Top with desired fruit topping or serve plain. Makes about 8 servings.

PUMPKIN CHEESECAKE

Crust:

1½ cups finely crushed graham cracker
    crumbs

3 tablespoons butter, melted

Filling:

3 (8-ounce) packages cream cheese,
    softened

1 cup granulated sugar

3 eggs

¾ teaspoon vanilla

1⅓ cups plus 2 tablespoons pumpkin

¾ teaspoon ground cinnamon

¼ teaspoon nutmeg

¼ teaspoon ground ginger

¼ teaspoon ground cloves

½ teaspoon salt

Topping:

2 cups sour cream

3 tablespoons granulated sugar

½ teaspoon vanilla

Preheat oven to 300 degrees.

Prepare Crust: Mix graham cracker crumbs and melted butter and press firmly onto bottom and sides of a 9- or 10-inch springform pan and set aside.

Prepare Filling: Beat cream cheese in the bowl of an electric mixer until smooth. Gradually add sugar, then eggs, one at a time, beating well after each addition. Stir in vanilla. In a separate bowl, combine pumpkin, cinnamon, nutmeg, ginger, cloves, and salt. Mix well and fold into cream cheese mixture. Pour filling into crust. Bake 55 minutes.

When cheesecake is almost finished baking, beat sour cream with a wire whisk; add sugar and vanilla and mix well. Spread on top of cheesecake and return to oven. Bake 10 more minutes. Cool before removing sides from springform pan. Garnish with a sprinkle of nutmeg. Refrigerate until ready to serve. Makes 10 to 12 servings.

GRASSHOPPER CHEESECAKE

Crust:
1½ cups slivered almonds

¼ cup powdered whey

2 tablespoons granulated sugar

¼ cup butter, melted

Ganache:
4.5 ounces bittersweet baking chocolate

¼ cup heavy cream

Filling:
3 (8-ounce) packages cream cheese, softened

¾ cup granulated sugar

¾ cup sour cream

1 teaspoon peppermint extract

Green food coloring, according to taste

4 eggs

Whipped cream, for garnish

Chocolate sauce, for garnish

Preheat oven to 350 degrees.

Prepare Crust: Place almonds in food processor fitted with an S-blade. Process until the almonds are a medium-fine texture. Add the whey and sugar and pulse once. Place the almond meal in a bowl and drizzle the melted butter into it. Mix with your hands until it feels slightly squishy.

Press into the bottom of a 10-inch springform pan. Bake 12 to 15 minutes, or until lightly browned and slightly pulling away from the sides of the pan. Remove from the oven and let crust cool while you make the ganache.

For Ganache: Melt chocolate with cream in the top of a double boiler over simmering water. Whisk well to make a smooth, shiny ganache. Spread evenly over the crust and set aside.

Reduce oven temperature to 325 degrees. Place a pan of water on bottom rack of oven.

For Filling: In a mixing bowl, beat the cream cheese until smooth, scraping down the sides of the bowl often. Beat in the sugar and the sour cream and mix well. Add peppermint extract and food coloring. Add eggs, one at a time, beating after each addition until very smooth and creamy.

Pour the mixture into the chocolate-coated crust. Place the cake in the oven, on the rack above the pan of water. Bake for 1 hour. Turn off the oven and prop the door open to cool the cake slowly for an hour and thus avoid the cake cracking.

Remove from oven and chill. Remove sides of pan and slice into 16 even pieces. Garnish with whipped cream and a drizzle of chocolate sauce.

Grasshopper Cheesecake

Banana Split Cake

Banana Split Cake

Crust:

2 cups graham cracker crumbs

½ cup butter or margarine, melted

Filling:

½ cup pasteurized eggs (enough to equal 2 eggs)

¾ cup butter or margarine, room temperature

2 cups powdered sugar

Topping:

4 large bananas

1 (20-ounce) can crushed pineapple, drained

1 (12-ounce) carton frozen whipped topping, thawed

1 bottle fudge ice cream topping

¼ cup chopped nuts

¼ cup maraschino cherries, quartered

To make the crust, mix together graham cracker crumbs and butter; press in the bottom of an ungreased 9 x 13-inch pan. Refrigerate 10 to 12 minutes.

Prepare filling: In a large bowl, beat together eggs, powdered sugar, and butter until light and fluffy, approximately 10 to 12 minutes. Spread filling on top of crumb mixture.

Slice the bananas on top of the filling; spread the crushed pineapple on top of the bananas. Spread the whipped topping on top of the pineapple. Warm the fudge topping slightly and drizzle on top of the whipped topping. Garnish the top with chopped nuts and cherries.

Refrigerate for at least 4 hours. For best results, refrigerate overnight. This dessert is very rich. Makes 15 servings.

Gingerbread

½ cup granulated sugar

½ cup butter, softened

1 egg, well beaten

1 cup molasses

½ teaspoon salt

2½ cups all-purpose flour

1½ teaspoons baking soda

1 teaspoon ground cinnamon

1 teaspoon ground ginger

½ teaspoon ground cloves

1 cup very hot water

Bananas, for garnishing

Whipped cream, for garnishing

Preheat oven to 350 degrees. Grease a 9 x 13-inch baking pan and set aside. In a large bowl, cream together butter and sugar. Add egg and molasses and beat well. Sift dry ingredients together and add to creamed mixture. Add hot water and beat until smooth (batter will be very thin). Pour into prepared baking pan. Bake 40 minutes or until cake tests done when a toothpick inserted near center comes out clean. Serve warm or cold topped with sliced bananas and whipped cream. Makes 16 servings.

Variation: Drain 1 (27-ounce) can pear halves and place pears, cut side down, on bottom of baking pan. Pour batter over top and bake as directed.

Pumpkin Cake Roll

3 eggs

1 cup granulated sugar

⅔ cup canned pumpkin

1 teaspoon lemon juice

¾ cup all-purpose flour

1 teaspoon baking powder

2 teaspoons ground cinnamon

1 teaspoon ground ginger

½ teaspoon nutmeg

½ teaspoon salt

½ cup chopped nuts

Powdered sugar

¼ cup margarine, softened

2 (3-ounce) packages cream cheese, softened

1 cup powdered sugar

½ teaspoon vanilla

Preheat oven to 350 degrees. Line a 10 x 15-inch jelly roll pan with parchment paper, grease paper, and set aside.

In a large bowl, beat eggs with an electric mixer until lemon colored. Gradually add sugar. Stir in pumpkin and lemon juice. In a separate bowl, sift together flour, baking powder, cinnamon, ginger, nutmeg, and salt; fold into egg-pumpkin mixture. Pour batter into prepared pan, smooth out top, and sprinkle with chopped nuts. Bake for 15 minutes.

Lay a clean kitchen towel out on the counter. Sprinkle powdered sugar on kitchen towel. Turn the warm cake onto towel and remove parchment paper. Roll up cake and towel lengthwise. Cool in refrigerator or freezer.

While cake cools, beat margarine and cream cheese together until smooth. Beat in 1 cup powdered sugar. Add vanilla. Unroll cake and spread with filling, then roll up again. Cut cake roll in half. Wrap each roll in plastic wrap until served. Store in refrigerator, or freeze for later use. Cut rolls into 1-inch slices to serve.

Rhubarb Cake

Topping:

¾ cup packed brown sugar

½ cup chopped walnuts

1½ teaspoons ground cinnamon

3 tablespoons butter

Cake:

1½ cups packed brown sugar

½ cup butter or shortening, softened

1 egg

1 cup milk

1 teaspoon vanilla

¼ teaspoon salt

1 teaspoon baking soda

1¾ cups all-purpose flour

3 cups chopped fresh rhubarb

Preheat oven to 350 degrees.

Prepare Topping: Combine brown sugar, nuts, and cinnamon in a small bowl. Cut in butter until crumbs form. Set mixture aside.

Prepare Cake: In a large bowl, cream together sugar and butter until fluffy. Add egg, milk, vanilla, salt, baking soda, and flour and beat well. Stir in rhubarb and mix thoroughly. Pour into a 9 x 13-inch pan and sprinkle with topping. Bake for 50 minutes. Serve warm with ice cream or whipped cream. Makes 12 to 14 servings.

Pumpkin Cake Roll

LEMON-LIME POKE CAKE

 QUICK & EASY

1 package lemon cake mix

⅓ cup all-purpose flour

½ cup vegetable oil

3 eggs

1 (3-ounce) package lime flavored gelatin

1½ cups boiling water

½ cup cold water

1 (3-ounce) package instant lemon pudding and pie filling

1 cup milk

1 (8-ounce) carton frozen nondairy whipped topping, thawed

Preheat oven to 350 degrees. Coat a 9 x 13-inch cake pan with cooking spray and set aside.

In a large bowl, blend dry cake mix, flour, vegetable oil, and eggs on low speed for 30 seconds. Increase speed to medium and beat for 2 minutes. Pour batter into prepared pan and spread out evenly. Bake 30 to 35 minutes or until toothpick inserted near center comes out clean.

While cake is baking, dissolve lime gelatin in boiling water. Add cold water and set aside.

While cake is hot, poke holes all over the surface of the cake with a meat fork. Slowly pour lime gelatin evenly over top of the cake. Refrigerate cake until cool, about 2 to 3 hours. When ready to serve, beat pudding mix into cold milk with a wire whisk until pudding starts to thicken. Fold in whipped topping and frost cake. Store finished cake in refrigerator. Makes 12 to 14 servings.

LEMON SURPRISE

 QUICK & EASY

1 package yellow or white cake mix, baked in a 9 x 13-inch pan according to high-altitude directions on box and cooled

1 (6-ounce) package cook-and-stir lemon pudding and pie mix, prepared according to package directions

1 (8-ounce) carton frozen nondairy whipped topping, thawed

Spread warm lemon pudding over top of cooled cake. Refrigerate several hours, until chilled. Before serving, spread whipped topping over pudding layer. Store cake in refrigerator. Makes 12 to 14 servings.

to 400 degrees. In a small saucepan, bring water to a boil. Add the flour all at once and stir rapidly re forms a ball. Remove from heat. With an elec- at eggs in the hot mixture, one at a time, beat- each addition. Spread dough on an ungreased cookie sheet. Bake 30 minutes. Cool. (Crust the moon's surface, which is how it gets its t prick, let stand as is.

wl, beat cream cheese until it is very soft. In l, mix the milk and pudding mix. Blend cream the pudding and mix together until smooth. crust and refrigerate 20 minutes.

y top with whipped topping. Drizzle with chocolate sprinkle with chopped nuts. Make 20 servings.

QUICK
& EASY

2 packages blueberry muffin mixes

½ cup packed brown sugar

½ cup chopped nuts

1 teaspoon ground cinnamon

2 eggs

1½ cups sour cream

1 cup water

½ cup powdered sugar

2 tablespoons milk

Preheat oven to 350 degrees. Grease a 12-cup Bundt pan and set aside.

Drain and rinse blueberries from muffin mixes and set aside. Combine brown sugar, nuts, and cinnamon in a small bowl and set aside.

In a large bowl, blend eggs, sour cream, and water. Add muffin mix. Stir with fork until well blended. Spread half of the batter in pan, top with sugar mixture and drained blueberries. Spread remaining batter on top.

Bake 50 minutes. While cake is still warm, beat powdered sugar and milk together until smooth. Turn out cake onto a serving platter and drizzle with glaze.

Luscious Layered Raspberry Delight

Luscious Layered Raspberry Delight

14 whole graham crackers
1 (3-ounce) package vanilla instant
    pudding
2 cups milk
1 cup frozen nondairy whipped
    topping, thawed
1 (21-ounce) can raspberry pie filling

Line a 9-inch square pan with whole graham crackers, breaking if necessary. Prepare pudding mix as directed, using 2 cups milk. Let stand 5 minutes, then blend in whipped topping. Spread half the pudding mixture over the crackers. Add another layer of crackers; top with the remaining pudding mixture and remaining crackers. Spread pie filling over top layer of crackers. Chill for 3 hours. Serves 9.

No-Bake Fruit Cake

1 (16-ounce) box vanilla wafers, crushed
1 (15-ounce) can sweetened condensed
    milk
2 cups chopped pecans
2 cups chopped walnuts
2 (8-ounce) packages chopped dates
1 pound candied cherries

Mix all ingredients together well. Divide mixture in half, placing each half on a piece of plastic wrap. Work into a roll, wrap in plastic wrap, and refrigerate. To serve, slice while cold and allow to come to room temperature. Makes 10 servings.

Cream Puffs and Éclairs

PUDDINGS, PASTRIES, AND FROZEN DESSERTS

Puff Pastries

1 cup all-purpose flour
¼ teaspoon salt
½ cup butter
1 cup boiling water
4 eggs

Preheat oven to 425 degrees. Line baking sheets with parchment paper.

Sift flour with salt in a small bowl. Combine butter and boiling water in a saucepan and cook on low heat until butter is melted. Add flour all at once and stir vigorously until mixture forms a ball and leaves sides of pan. Cook about 2 minutes, until mixture is very dry. Remove from heat. Add unbeaten eggs one at a time, beating well after each addition. Continue beating until a thick dough forms. For cream puffs, drop dough by tablespoonfuls onto prepared baking sheets, about 2 inches apart. (See variations below and on page 124 for other baking directions.) Bake about 15 minutes. Reduce heat to 375 degrees and bake for 15 more minutes. Bake about 30 to 40 minutes total, or until beads of moisture no longer appear on surface. Do not open oven door during early part of baking. Remove to wire racks to cool. When cool, cut slit in side of each puff; remove doughy centers, if necessary. Makes about 12 large cream puff shells.

Cocktail Puffs

Prepare dough as directed above. Drop dough by very small teaspoonfuls onto prepared baking sheets. Bake 17 to 20 minutes. Fill with any savory filling. Makes 4 to 5 dozen small puffs.

Cream Puffs

Prepare puff pastries as directed on page 123. Remove dough centers and fill with your favorite pudding or sweetened whipped cream.

Éclairs

Prepare puff pastries as directed on page 123. Instead of dropping dough onto baking sheets, force it through a decorating tube in strips about 1-inch wide and 4-inches long. Bake about 25 minutes. Fill as for cream puffs. Frost with your favorite chocolate frosting. Makes about 18 éclairs.

Puff Shells

Prepare dough as directed on page 123. Drop dough from tablespoon into deep hot fat (375 degrees). Fry 10 to 15 seconds or until a good crust forms, turning often. Drain well, then cut top off each shell. Fill hot shells with creamed fish, poultry, meat, eggs, or vegetables. Or cool shells and fill with a salad mixture. Replace tops before serving. Makes about 12 large shells.

CHOCOLATE PARTY PUFFS

60 Cocktail Puffs, baked but unfilled (see recipe on page 123)
1 quart vanilla ice cream
1 quart heavy cream, whipped
1 tablespoon granulated sugar, or to taste
1 teaspoon vanilla, or to taste
1 cup chocolate syrup
1 (16-ounce) jar maraschino cherries, well-drained

Slit cooled puffs and pull out any dough strands inside. Fill shells with vanilla ice cream. Freeze filled shells on a tray in a single layer. Once frozen, pack shells in plastic bags and store in freezer until ready to use.

When ready to serve, whip cream. Stir in sugar, vanilla, and chocolate syrup. Fold slightly thawed puffs and cherries into cream. Layer into a glass trifle bowl and serve immediately. Makes 20 servings of 3 puffs each, or 15 servings of 4 puffs each.

BREAD PUDDING

10 slices bread (any variety) or Lion
    House Dinner Rolls
½ cup butter
¾ to 1 cup raisins
6 eggs
6 cups milk (whole milk recommended)
¾ cup granulated sugar
Pinch salt
¾ teaspoon vanilla
¾ teaspoon nutmeg, plus more for dust-
    ing top of pudding
1 recipe Lemon Butter Sauce (see below)

Preheat oven to 350 degrees. Coat a 9 x 13-inch pan with nonstick cooking spray and set aside. Cut off crusts from bread. Place one layer of bread slices in pan and brush with melted butter. Sprinkle raisins on top. Place another layer of bread on top of raisins and brush with melted butter.

In a large bowl, mix eggs, milk, sugar, salt, vanilla, and ¾ teaspoon nutmeg with wire whisk. Pour over bread. Sprinkle nutmeg over top of pudding and allow to set for 30 to 45 minutes. Bake 45 minutes, or until custard is formed and knife inserted near center comes out clean. Serve topped with Lemon Butter Sauce. Serves 16.

Variation: 2 cups fresh or frozen raspberries can be substituted for raisins and vanilla buttersauce for lemon.

Lemon Butter Sauce

2 cups granulated sugar
¼ cup plus ½ teaspoon cornstarch
¼ teaspoon salt
2 cups water
1 cup butter, cut in small pieces
1½ teaspoons lemon extract

Place sugar, cornstarch, and salt in a 4-quart saucepan and stir until blended. Add water. Bring to a boil and cook 5 minutes, stirring constantly. Remove from heat; stir in butter and lemon extract until butter is melted and mixture is creamy. Makes 4 cups.

Variation: Omit lemon extract and add 2 teaspoons vanilla extract.

CARAMEL BREAD PUDDING

4 to 5 Lion House Dinner Rolls or other
    large, soft rolls
½ cup packed brown sugar
½ cup butter
1 cup cream or half and half
1 teaspoon vanilla
2 eggs, beaten

Preheat oven to 350 degrees. Tear rolls into pieces and put in a baking dish coated with cooking spray (a medium casserole dish works well).

Melt the brown sugar and butter in a small saucepan over medium-low heat. Take the pan off the heat and whisk in the cream, vanilla, and beaten eggs. Pour over the rolls and let rest for 10 minutes. Bake 20 minutes. Makes 6 to 8 servings.

RICE PUDDING

2 cups milk (whole milk recommended)

1 (5-ounce) can evaporated milk

½ cup plus 2 tablespoons granulated
    sugar

2 eggs, slightly beaten

¼ teaspoon salt

1 tablespoon cornstarch

2 cups cooked rice

½ cup raisins

⅛ teaspoon nutmeg

⅛ teaspoon ground cinnamon

1 teaspoon vanilla

Place 1½ cups of the milk, the evaporated milk, and 6 tablespoons of the sugar in top of a double boiler. Heat until milk is scalded. In mixing bowl, whisk eggs; add salt and remaining 4 tablespoons sugar and whisk again. Slowly pour egg mixture into scalded milk, stirring constantly with wire whisk. Cook 15 to 20 minutes, stirring occasionally. In a small bowl, mix reserved ½ cup milk and cornstarch; slowly pour into milk mixture, stirring constantly until pudding begins to thicken. (Stir constantly or lumps will form.) Stir thoroughly and cook 10 to 15 more minutes, or until cornstarch flavor is gone. Add cooked rice and cook 7 more minutes. Remove from heat and add raisins, nutmeg, cinnamon, and vanilla. Serves 8.

Note: If double boiler is not available, place a stainless steel bowl on top of small saucepan of boiling water, or cook pudding in a heavy saucepan, stirring constantly. (Cooking time will be less in a saucepan.)

CREAMY TAPIOCA PUDDING

3 tablespoons quick-cooking tapioca

5 tablespoons granulated sugar, divided

⅛ teaspoon salt

2 cups milk (whole milk recommended)

1 egg, separated

¾ teaspoon vanilla

In a small saucepan, mix tapioca, 3 tablespoons of the sugar, salt, milk, and egg yolk. Let stand while preparing meringue. Beat egg white until foamy. Add 2 tablespoons sugar and beat until soft peaks form. Let stand while cooking pudding.

Cook tapioca mixture over medium heat to full boil, stirring constantly (6 to 8 minutes). Gradually pour hot mixture into beaten egg white, stirring quickly to blend. Stir in vanilla and cool slightly. Stir. Serve warm or chilled; garnish as desired. Makes 5 servings.

Rice Pudding

Chocolate Decadence

CHOCOLATE DECADENCE

1 (12-ounce) package semi-sweet
    chocolate chips
4 ounces unsweetened chocolate,
    chopped
1½ cups butter, melted
½ cup water
1¾ cups granulated sugar
7 eggs
2 cups whipped cream

Preheat oven to 350 degrees. Place a pan of water on the bottom rack of oven. Line a 10-inch round pan with parchment paper and grease lightly. Place chocolate chips and chopped chocolate in a medium bowl. Place butter, water, and 1½ cups of the sugar in a medium saucepan and bring to a boil over medium heat. Stir to combine, then pour over the chocolate and let the mixture rest until smooth. Whip the eggs with the remaining ¼ cup sugar until thick; fold into the chocolate mixture and pour into prepared pan. Bake 40 to 50 minutes on rack above the pan of water. Dessert is done when a toothpick inserted near center comes out clean. Allow to cool, then spread with whipped cream, and serve. Makes 10 servings.

Note: This recipe is easy to freeze for use at a later time. Simply, cool, chill in refrigerator, then freeze.

CHOCOLATE DREAM BARS

8 graham crackers, finely crushed
¼ cup butter, melted
1 (8-ounce) package cream cheese,
    softened
1 cup powdered sugar
¾ cup chocolate chips, melted
¼ cup chocolate syrup (such as
    Hershey's®)
1 cup whipping cream
1 cup sweetened whipped cream,
    for garnish
Chocolate chips, for garnish

Coat a 9 x 9-inch pan with cooking spray and set aside.

Combine crushed graham crackers and melted butter in a small bowl, then press into prepared pan and set aside.

In a medium bowl, beat cream cheese and powdered sugar until smooth. Mix in the cooled, melted chocolate chips and the chocolate syrup. Mix well. Whip cream and fold into cream cheese mixture.

Spoon the mixture on top of the graham crust and refrigerate. Chill 3 hours or overnight.

To serve, cut into squares and top each with a dollop of sweetened whipped cream and a few chocolate chips. Makes about 9 servings.

WHITE MOUSSE

1 (1-pound) package Oreo® cookies
½ cup butter, melted
1½ cups white chocolate chips
½ cup heavy cream
1 (16-ounce) carton frozen nondairy
    whipped topping, thawed
Chocolate curls, for garnishing
Fresh berries, for garnishing

Place cookies in the bowl of a food processor and process until they become fine crumbs. Place in a separate bowl. Pour melted butter over the crumbs and mix thoroughly. Press crumbs into an 8-inch springform pan. Freeze 1 hour.

In a small saucepan over low heat, melt white chocolate chips with cream until cream almost scalds. Remove from heat and allow to cool slightly. Stir well to form a white ganache. It may look lumpy at first, but keep stirring until it looks smooth and beautiful.

Place thawed whipped topping in the bowl of a large mixer and whip in the ganache.

Fill the crust with the white mousse, smoothing top from the center outward. Freeze until solid, usually overnight. Garnish with chocolate curls and fresh berries. Makes 14 to 16 servings.

SWEET AND SALTY ICE CREAM PIE

2 quarts vanilla ice cream
1 (1-pound) package Oreo® cookies
½ (11-ounce) bottle hot fudge sauce
½ (11-ounce) bottle caramel ice cream
    topping
1½ cups peanuts, salted without skins
½ bag miniature marshmallows

Allow the ice cream to soften slightly, enough to stir but not runny. Coarsely crush Oreo cookies so there are both large and small chunks. Remove 1½ cups of crumbs and crush until they are finely ground. (Reserve remaining crumbs to mix into the ice cream later.) Sprinkle half of the finely crushed crumbs in the bottom of a 9 x 13-inch cake pan.

Spoon ice cream into a large bowl and stir. Add the larger cookie crumbs and the marshmallows and stir together. Working quickly, place half of this mixture on top of the crumbs in the cake pan. Sprinkle the peanuts on top and drizzle the hot fudge sauce (not warmed) and caramel topping over the peanuts. Place the remaining ice cream mixture on top and spread evenly. Sprinkle the remaining finely crushed cookie crumbs on top of the ice cream and return to the freezer for at least 3 hours. This can be made up to 2 weeks in advance.

To serve, remove from freezer and allow to set out for 10 minutes. Cut in desired size pieces. Makes 16 to 18 servings.

COOKING HELPS

COMMON FOOD EQUIVALENTS

FOOD	AMOUNT	APPROXIMATE EQUIVALENT
Cheese, hard	4 ounces	1 cup, shredded
Cheese, cottage	1 pound	2 cups
Cheese, cream	3-ounce package	6 tablespoons
Cheese, cream	8-ounce package	1 cup
Chocolate chips	12-ounce package	2 cups
Cream, sour	8-ounce carton	1 cup
Cream, whipping	½ pint	1 cup (2 cups whipped)
Flour, all-purpose	1 pound	3½ cups
Flour, cake	1 pound	4 cups
Sugar, brown	1 pound	2¼ cups
Sugar, granulated	1 pound	2 cups
Sugar, powdered	1 pound	4 cups
Lemon juice	1 medium lemon	2 to 3 tablespoons
Margarine or Butter	1 pound	2 cups
Margarine or Butter	1 stick	½ cup
Onion	1 medium	½ cup chopped
Orange juice	1 medium orange	⅓ to ½ cup
Egg noodles, uncooked	8 ounces	4 to 5 cups cooked
Macaroni, uncooked	2 cups	4 cups cooked
Spaghetti, uncooked	8 ounces	4 cups cooked

EVERYDAY EQUIVALENTS

WHOLE FOOD	=	CHOPPED, SLICED, DICED, OR CRUSHED FOOD
Apples, 1 pound	=	3 medium or 3 cups, sliced
Bananas, 1 pound	=	3 to 4 medium or 2 cups, mashed
Berries, 1 basket	=	1¾ cups
3 to 4 slices dry bread	=	1 cup fine crumbs
1 slice soft bread	=	¾ cup soft crumbs
12 graham cracker squares	=	1 cup fine crumbs
21 saltine cracker squares	=	1 cup fine crumbs
9 pieces zwieback	=	1 cup fine crumbs
26 to 30 vanilla wafers	=	1 cup fine crumbs
1 ounce butter	=	2 tablespoons
1 stick butter	=	½ cup
1 pound butter	=	2 cups
Candied fruit, 8 ounces	=	1½ cups
Cheese, cheddar, 8 ounces	=	1 cup grated
3-ounce package cream cheese	=	6 tablespoons
8-ounce package cream cheese	=	16 tablespoons
Cocoa, 4 ounces	=	1 cup
Coconut, shredded, 1 pound	=	5 cups
Cranberries, 1 pound	=	3 to 3½ cups sauce
Cream, whipping, 1 cup	=	2 cups whipped
Dates, 1 pound	=	2½ cups or 1¾ cups pitted
1 cup dried lima beans	=	2½ cups cooked
1 cup dried beans	=	2 cups cooked
1 cup dried white beans	=	3 cups cooked
1 cup dried split peas	=	2½ cups cooked
Egg whites, 4	=	½ cup
Egg yolks, 6	=	½ cup
Eggs, 1 cup	=	4 or 5 large or 6 or 7 medium

Everyday Equivalents

WHOLE FOOD	=	CHOPPED, SLICED, DICED, OR CRUSHED FOOD
All-purpose flour, 1 pound	=	4 cups sifted
Bread flour, 1 pound	=	4 cups
Cake flour, 1 pound	=	4¾ cups sifted
Whole Wheat flour, 1 pound	=	3½ cups
Honey, 1 pound	=	1⅓ cups
Lemon, 1 medium	=	¾ tablespoon juice and 1 to 1½ tablespoons rind
Macaroni, 7- or 8-ounce package	=	4 cups cooked
1 cup miniature marshmallows	=	11 large marshmallows
1 large marshmallow	=	10 miniature marshmallows
Evaporated milk, small can	=	⅔ cup
Evaporated milk, large can	=	1⅔ cup
Sweetened condensed milk, can	=	1⅓ cups
Noodles, 4 ounces (1½ to 2 cups)	=	2 cups cooked
Almonds, 1 pound	=	1¾ cups
1 pound shelled almonds	=	3½ cups
Pecans, 1 pound	=	2½ cups
1 pound, shelled pecans	=	4 cups
Peanuts, 1 pound	=	3 cups
1 pound, shelled peanuts	=	2¼ cups
Walnuts, 1 pound	=	1⅔ cups
1 pound shelled walnuts	=	4 cups
Oatmeal, 1 pound	=	5 cups raw or 10 cups cooked
Orange, 1 medium	=	⅓ to ½ cup juice or 1 to 2 tablespoons rind
Potatoes, Sweet, 1 pound	=	3 cups sliced or 3 medium
Potatoes, white, 1 pound	=	2½ cups sliced or 2 cups mashed
Raisins, 15-ounce package	=	3 cups

EVERYDAY EQUIVALENTS

WHOLE FOOD	=	CHOPPED, SLICED, DICED, OR CRUSHED FOOD
⅓ cup regular white rice	=	1 cup cooked
¼ cup converted or brown rice	=	1 cup cooked
½ cup instant rice	=	1 cup cooked
1 pound regular rice, 2½ cups	=	8 cups cooked
Spaghetti, 7- or 8-ounce package	=	4 cups cooked
Brown sugar, 1 pound	=	2¼ cups
Granulated sugar, 1 pound	=	2 cups
Powdered sugar, 1 pound	=	4½ cups sifted

GUIDE TO KITCHEN PANS

IF RECIPE CALLS FOR:	USE EITHER:
4-cup baking dish	9-inch pie pan or 8-inch round cake pan or 8 x 4-inch loaf pan
6-cup baking dish	9-inch round cake pan or 10-inch pie pan or 8 x 4-inch loaf pan
8-cup baking dish	8-inch square pan or 11 x 7-inch pan or 9 x 5-inch loaf pan
10-cup baking dish	9-inch square pan or 12 x 8-inch baking pan or 15 x 10-inch jelly roll pan
12-cup baking dish	9 x 13-inch pan

MEASUREMENTS

EQUIVALENT MEASURES:

3 teaspoons	=	1 tablespoon
4 tablespoons	=	¼ cup
5 tablespoons + 1 teaspoon	=	⅓ cup
8 tablespoons	=	½ cup
10 tablespoons + 2 teaspoons	=	⅔ cup
12 tablespoons	=	¾ cup
16 tablespoons	=	1 cup = 8 fluid ounces
2 cups	=	1 pint = 16 fluid ounces
4 cups	=	2 pints = 1 quart = 32 fluid ounces
2 quarts	=	½ gallon = 64 fluid ounces
4 quarts	=	1 gallon = 128 fluid ounces

METRIC CONVERSIONS:

VOLUME CONVERSIONS:

1 milliliter	=	slightly less than ¼ teaspoon
2 milliliters	=	slightly less than ½ teaspoon
5 milliliters	=	1 teaspoon
15 milliliters	=	1 tablespoon
59 milliliters	=	¼ cup
79 milliliters	=	⅓ cup
237 milliliters	=	1 cup
0.946 liter	=	4 cups = 1 quart
1 liter	=	1.06 quarts
3.8 liters	=	4 quarts = 1 gallon

WEIGHT CONVERSIONS:

28 grams	=	1 ounce
113 grams	=	4 ounces
227 grams	=	8 ounces
454 grams	=	16 ounces = 1 pound

SUBSTITUTIONS (Recipe results will vary when using substitutions. Use only in emergency circumstances.)

MISSING	AMOUNT	REPLACE WITH
Powdered sugar	1 cup	1 cup granulated + 1 teaspoon cornstarch, mixed in blender
Unsweetened chocolate	1 ounce	3 tablespoons cocoa powder + 1 tablespoons vegetable oil OR 1½ ounces bittersweet chocolate (remove 1 tablespoon sugar from recipe)
Bittersweet chocolate	1 ounce	4 tablespoons cocoa powder + 2 tablespoons butter OR ⅔ ounce unsweetened chocolate + 2 teaspoons sugar
Milk	1 cup	½ cup evaporated milk + ½ cup water OR ¼ cup nonfat dry milk + ⅞ cup water + 2 teaspoons butter
Buttermilk	1 cup	1 cup milk + 1 tablespoon lemon juice (stir together and let sit 5 minutes before use)
Whole milk	1 cup	⅝ skim milk + ⅜ cup half and half OR ⅔ cup 1% milk + ⅓ cup half and half OR ¾ cup 2% milk + ¼ cup half and half
Half and half	1 cup	¾ cup whole milk + ¼ cup heavy cream OR ⅔ cup skim or lowfat milk + ⅓ cup heavy cream
Cornstarch (for thickening)	1 tablespoon	2 tablespoons flour
Flour (for thickening)	1 tablespoon	½ to ⅔ tablespoon cornstarch
Cake flour	1 cup	⅞ cup all-purpose flour + 2 tablespoons cornstarch
Self-rising flour	1 cup	1 cup all-purpose flour + 1½ teaspoons baking powder + ½ teaspoon salt
Baking powder	1 teaspoon	¼ teaspoon baking soda + ½ teaspoon cream of tartar
Minced onion	2 tablespoons	1 teaspoon onion powder
Tomato juice	1 cup	½ cup tomato sauce + ½ cup water
Tomato sauce	2 cups	¾ cup tomato paste + 1 cup water

INDEX